BECOMING A
Dallas Cowboys
CHEERLEADER

*40 Lessons on Faith
I Learned Along the Way*

Carolyn Clifton Hill

Copyright © 2025 Carolyn Clifton Hill

All rights reserved. No part of this book may be reproduced, stored in a retrieval system, or transmitted in any form or by any means—electronic, mechanical, photocopying, recording, or otherwise—without prior written permission from the author, except for brief quotations used in reviews or articles.

Publisher: Strong Foundation Publishing
ISBN: 979-8-218-84574-2

Scripture taken predominantly from the Holy Bible, New International Version® (NIV), © 1973, 1978, 1984, 2011 by Biblica, Inc.® All rights reserved worldwide. The "NIV" and "New International Version" are registered trademarks of Biblica, Inc., in the United States Patent and Trademark Office. Other Scripture references include brief excerpts from The Message, The Passion Translation, Contemporary English Version, New Living Translation, and various other paraphrases. All Scripture quotations are used for devotional and inspirational purposes and are not intended for commercial sale outside this work.

Certain song lyrics quoted in this book are included for educational, devotional, or inspirational purposes. All rights to the quoted lyrics are held by the respective copyright owners. No lyrics are used for commercial purposes outside this work.

Book Cover Design: Connor Hill

Photo Credits and Disclaimer:
All photographs included in this book are from the personal collection of the author or are royalty free images and are used solely to illustrate her own experiences. The appearance of any individual, including public figures, is incidental to the author's personal story and does not imply endorsement or participation in this publication.

This book is a personal memoir and reflection of the author's experiences as a former Dallas Cowboys Cheerleader. It is not authorized, endorsed, or sponsored by the Dallas Cowboys organization or the Dallas Cowboys Cheerleaders organization. Any photographs from the author's time as a Dallas Cowboys Cheerleader included in this book are personal photos, used solely to illustrate the author's individual story. All opinions and perspectives expressed are also solely the author's.

For my parents,

Joe and Kay Clifton—now in heaven with Jesus.

I will always remember their voices, rising above the roar of the crowd—cheering for the Cowboys, and cheering even louder for little ol' me. Their faith and love planted seeds in my heart that, by God's grace, continue to grow today.

Acknowledgements

To my husband, Jerod—You are the one and only love of my life. Your servant's heart reflects the love of Christ so purely. You lead with quiet strength, give with gracious humility, and love with a depth that reaches my soul. This book exists because you trusted what God could do through it, even when I wavered. You have cheered for me, sacrificed for me, and prayed over me more times than I could ever count. I thank God every single day for the gift of you. I love you—fully, endlessly, and beyond what words could ever hold.

To my boys, Connor and Dylan—You two are the greatest joys God has ever given me. It fills my heart with indescribable thankfulness to witness you becoming the faithful, remarkable young men God created you to be. Thank you for your hugs when I needed encouragement, and for reminding me—just by being yourselves—what really matters in life. Your wit, integrity, and strength inspire me more than you know. Being your Mom is, without question, my greatest dream come true. Love you BIG, always and forever!

To my sister, Kathryn—You're my lifelong best friend, beautiful role model, and faithful protector. From the moment I was born, you have been my hero! I don't know what I would do without your wisdom, love, and unwavering support. Your prayers have carried me, your honesty has guided me, and your presence has been a safe place in every season. You are a gift I will never stop thanking God for. I love you—and your amazing family—with all my heart.

To my friend, Bonnie Cunningham—Thank you for lovingly and persistently challenging me to write a devotional book. Your belief in me gave me the courage to begin. You saw something in me that I couldn't yet see, and I am forever grateful! The time and care you devoted to this project is a precious gift I will never forget. I love you and deeply appreciate your gracious and generous heart.

To my friend, Sundi Jo Graham—Thank you for being the one who encouraged me to write about my Dallas Cowboys Cheerleader days. Your insights and creative ideas shaped this book into something far greater than I could have ever imagined. You worked tirelessly behind the scenes—formatting, co-editing, and refining every detail—and went above and beyond in every way. You played an integral role in God's plan, a plan through which His healing love flowed as I wrote my story. He uses you so powerfully, and I'm so inspired by you! Your sincere prayers and steadfast friendship have meant the world to me. I love you to the moon and back—and around again!

To ALL of my precious friends, family, and faithful prayer warriors, you know who you are—Thank you for surrounding me with your love, encouragement, and intercession throughout this journey. Your prayers lifted me when I was weary, your words cheered me on when I needed strength, and your friendship reminded me I was never walking this road alone. Every page of this book carries the quiet power of your support and the covering of your prayers. I thank God for each of you—what a gift you are to my life. Much love to you all!

To my DCC mentor, Anita Jefferson Conley—Thank you for believing in me and showing me that I could become a Dallas Cowboys Cheerleader. Your heartfelt encouragement inspired me to believe it was possible, and your guidance and mentorship over the years became one of the greatest gifts of my journey. You are a rare and priceless jewel, and I love, appreciate, and admire you more than words can say!

To my dance and drill instructors, Durann Ardis and Pam Cole—Thank you for believing in me during my formative years. Durann, your passion to share the art of dance inspired me not only as a performer, but in every part of my life. Pam, your leadership shaped my character in ways that continue to bless me today. The confidence you both instilled, and the foundation you helped build, still echo in every step I take. I'm forever grateful for your kindness and for the role each of you played in preparing me for the path ahead. Love ya'll dearly!

To my DCC Director, Kelli Finglass, and Choreographer, Judy Trammell—Thank you for giving me the opportunity of a lifetime! Your leadership, vision, and dedication shaped not only an iconic organization but also the lives of countless young women, including mine. I'm deeply honored and forever grateful to have been part of something so extraordinary under your guidance. I sincerely love and appreciate you both!

To my beautiful DCC sisters I had the honor of cheering alongside— What a joy it was to share the field, endure the long rehearsals, and treasure the unforgettable moments with you. You are strong, talented, driven, and full of heart. I carry so many sweet memories from our time together, and I'm thankful for a sisterhood that lasts far beyond the uniform. I love every single one of you!

Above all, I give thanks and glory to my Lord and Savior, Jesus Christ —You are the Author of my story, the Giver of every good gift, and the steady hand that has guided me through every high and low. Thank You for the calling, the strength, the open doors, and even the detours that led me closer to You. This book is a reflection of Your faithfulness in my life, and my deepest prayer is that it points others back to You. May every word bring You glory.

Table of Contents

Introduction — 1

Lessons Learned:

1. God Alone Is Worthy Of Our Worship — 2
2. God Directs Our Steps — 7
3. People's Rejection Brings God's Redirection — 10
4. God Loves Us Because He Just Does — 13
5. What God Opens No One Can Shut, And What He Shuts No One Can Open — 18
6. The Truth Will Set You Free — 23
7. God's Mercy Is New Every Morning — 27
8. Comparison Does Not Define You — 31
9. With God, All Things Are Possible — 35
10. True Peace Is Trusting That God Is In Control — 38
11. When It's All About Me, Happiness Will Flee — 41
12. Waiting On The Lord Is Worth It — 44
13. Preparation Today Is What You'll Be Thankful For Tomorrow — 48
14. God Brings Purpose From Pain — 52
15. God Sees Your Potential — 55
16. God Has A Deeper Purpose For You Than Meets The Eye — 58
17. God Blesses Unity — 61
18. Always Keep Your Eyes On Jesus — 64
19. Doing Things God's Way Takes Determination — 67
20. Be A Student Of Those Around You — 71

21. Dedicate Everything You Do To The Lord	75
22. Be Concerned With What Concerns God	78
23. Kindness Is Key	82
24. Be Gracious, You Don't Know What People May Be Facing	85
25. God Wants To Work Through All Of Us	88
26. God Works All Things For Good For Those Who Love Him	91
27. Honor The Ones Who Sacrifice For You	94
28. Take Time To Remember What God Has Done	98
29. Boundaries Exist to Protect You	101
30. Be Respectful Toward Those Who See Things Differently	105
31. Make Loving Deposits In The Lives Of Others	109
32. Focus On The Real Things Of God	113
33. When We Are Real, We Begin To Heal	116
34. Store Up Treasures In Heaven	119
35. Move Boldly Toward The Dreams God's Placed In Your Heart	123
36. With God, Overcome The Wounds Of Words	128
37. Forgiveness Is God's Way	133
38. Always Show Gratitude For Your Family And Friends	137
39. Give Your Best Yes	140
40. You Are Enough In Christ Jesus	143
First Steps in Walking with Jesus	148
About the Author	151

Introduction

My Dad used to grin and call me his "lil' singin' and dancin' gal," and he wasn't wrong. I couldn't keep my soul from singing or my feet from dancing if I tried! Growing up in Texas, I performed anywhere I could —whether in small-town Opry Houses or beneath the Friday night lights. But from the very beginning, my heart was set on one dream: becoming a Dallas Cowboys Cheerleader.

That dream remained steady in me and never faded. But the road to making it a reality? It was anything but easy.

Through every twist and turn of my journey with the DCC, God was there—teaching me, shaping me, and gently shifting my gaze to Him. Over time, I came to realize it wasn't about achieving a dream. It was about learning to take my eyes off of myself and what the world told me mattered most. It was about learning to worship Him fully and freely. The process of becoming a DCC did more than give me a uniform—it transformed me into a cheerleader of another kind: one who will never stop cheering for my faithful Father God!

I believe God is calling me to share the lessons He's etched into my heart—lessons of faith, redemption, grace, hope, and His relentless love. You may recognize pieces of your own story in mine: the ache of feeling like you're not enough, the battle to believe God's truth over the world's lies, and the longing to know who you are in Christ. Through it all, He renews our minds, secures our identity in Him, and reveals who He truly is through His powerful love.

My prayer is that these lessons will be a rallying cry for your soul... that they'll remind you who you are, whose you are, and just how worthy He is of all our worship. Keep your eyes on Him, precious reader, and never stop cheering for the One who's always cheering for you.

Lesson 1
GOD ALONE IS WORTHY OF OUR WORSHIP

A sweet moment with my family at the DCC alumni reunion... grateful for God's faithfulness in every season.

"For great is the Lord our God and most worthy of praise; He is awesome above all gods."

1 Chronicles 16:25

I remember it... like it was last Sunday: waiting in the tunnel at the bottom of Texas Stadium, my heart pounding as I caught a glimpse of the massive crowd. Blue and silver shimmered in every direction, rising like a living wave into the sky. The atmosphere was pure electricity—and I was standing in the very crux of it.

Adrenaline surged through my body as the announcer's voice boomed: "And now, ladies and gentlemen, here they are—America's

Sweethearts! The often imitated, never equaled, internationally acclaimed, Dallas Cowboys Cheerleaders!"

"Go! Go! Go!" The music thundered, shaking me to my core until I could hardly breathe. Then, like a spark igniting a flame, we burst onto the field—lights blazing, cameras flashing, and a roar so powerful it seemed to lift us off the ground. In that storm of sound and color, we poured out everything we had—and then more.

When we truly believe in who we're cheering for, our passion proportionately escalates.

Long before I ever wore the DCC uniform, I was a child of Cowboys Nation. To me, it was more than football—being a super-fan was a tradition in our family, threaded deep into the fabric of who I was. I chased the dream of becoming an actual part of the Dallas Cowboys with everything in me, and after years of sweat, sacrifice, and grit, I finally earned my place on the squad.

Interestingly, while I was living it, the pressure that came with the position—and the praise—was harder to handle than I ever anticipated. In trying to relieve the weight of it all, I found myself caught in a painful cycle of binge eating and then starving myself. Looking back, I realize I was using food as a form of self-medication, and a way to grasp for control when things felt overwhelming.

And yet, I do not regret one moment of becoming a DCC. Not at all! It was a season that yielded unforgettable memories, lifelong friendships, and priceless life lessons. I'm *blown away* that the Lord allowed me to experience such an extraordinary chapter in my life. But one thing I've learned: No one handles that kind of attention well... when we try to keep it for ourselves.

We've all seen headlines about celebrities crumbling under the pressure of success and fame. The truth is, people were never meant to be placed on a pedestal. Nobody can live up to it, and when we idolize others, we will always be disappointed.

> **NO ONE HANDLES THAT KIND OF ATTENTION WELL... WHEN WE TRY TO KEEP IT FOR OURSELVES.**

Let me be clear: It's not wrong for people to be successful, famous, or powerful. God can use those qualities for His great purposes. But it's crucial to remember that all of it belongs to Him. Every gift, every breath, every opportunity—He is the source. When people reflect His glory and point it all back to Him, it benefits everyone.

One of my favorite Bible heroes, King David, understood this principle. He was ultra successful, famous, and powerful, but he gave God *all* of the praise and glory. In 2 Samuel chapter 6, he worshipped by "dancing with all his might before the Lord." His wife, Michal, did not get it. She mocked him. But David replied:

> "I will celebrate before the Lord. I will become even more undignified than this..."

You know, it's considered normal to scream your lungs out for a touchdown or lose your mind at a concert—but lift your hands in worship? Dance before the Lord? People might think you've lost it. But David didn't care. Because his praise wasn't about what people thought. It was about the greatness of God.

When we truly believe in *Who we are worshipping*, our passion proportionately escalates.

Do we passionately worship God?

It's not about performance. It's not about feelings. It's about loving God with all our heart, soul, mind, and strength. And we grow into that kind of love the more time we spend with Him. As our worship deepens, it becomes passionate and authentic. We can't contain it! In that place, we finally understand that God alone deserves to sit on the throne of our hearts.

The Lord made this lesson unmistakably clear when I returned to Dallas for a DCC reunion performance. I stood on that gigantic field, surrounded by all the fanfare—but this time I raised my sparkling silver pom-poms to the sky and worshipped my Lord and Savior with everything I had—and then more! What a moment of revelation and God's faithfulness. I had the best time! I felt totally secure and free in His love. Because when it's all about God—that's where joy lives.

So, if you're searching for excitement, fulfillment, belonging, or a chance to be a part of something bigger than yourself... and when worldly success still leaves you feeling empty... know this: Only God can fill that longing within you. He alone is worthy of our worship, and He is the One who will fill every empty space.

He did it for me, and I know He wants to do it for each and every one of us. I pray that my story, shared in the pages that follow, will encourage you to seek Him first, always. He is so worthy.

> "Seek the Kingdom of God above all else, and live righteously, and He will give you everything you need." - Matthew 6:33 (NLT)

Prayer

Lord, You alone are worthy of all my worship. Help me to keep my heart centered on You and to live every day in awe of who You are. I am so thankful for Your love, and I love You more than anything. May everything I say and do today be for Your glory.

In Jesus' Name, Amen.

Reflection

How can you grow more passionate in your worship of God? Is He truly sitting on the throne of your heart?

Lesson 2
GOD DIRECTS OUR STEPS

With my precious mentor and friend, Miss Anita.

"A man's steps are established by the Lord, and He takes pleasure in his way."
Psalm 37:23

When I was just five years old, I became absolutely fascinated with my neighbor's deck of Dallas Cowboys Cheerleaders playing cards. One of the cheerleaders in that deck stood out to me—Anita Jefferson. She reminded me of sunshine... and I wanted to grow up to be just like her.

And let me just pause right here and say: God and His ways are truly magnificent. It was no coincidence that ten years later, at age fifteen, the Lord orchestrated a divine connection—one that only He could arrange. I met Miss Anita.

To my amazement, she owned Danceline Co. in Dallas, where my high school drill team began attending camp and competitions. Anita took me under her wing and eventually gave me a job as one of her choreographers and dance instructors. I'll never forget sitting across from her at The Four Seasons—a very fancy place for this small-town girl—as we talked about exciting plans ahead. I remember thinking, "How is this even real right now?" It felt as if I had stepped into a realm of endless possibility.

Anita was fun-loving and full of life, yet also a strong Christian role model. I was deeply impacted by how she genuinely loved and encouraged all of us girls. Being a part of her Danceline Co. wasn't just about winning awards—it was about shaping hearts. She truly lived out Romans 12:10:

> *"Love each other with genuine affection, and take delight in honoring each other."*

Anita showed me that my dream wasn't out of reach—in fact, I could follow her example and pursue it in a way that honored God. When the time came for me to become a DCC, she was a voice of invaluable wisdom and support. And while I was cheering, she even blessed me with extra income by hiring me as her daughter's voice coach. Her kindness, generosity, and encouragement went far beyond anything I could have expected.

Through Anita, I learned how powerful it is to invest in others:

- Believe in people and walk with them in their journey.
- Speak life and encouragement through both words and actions.
- Share God's love freely and joyfully.

At the time, I loved and appreciated her. But looking back now, I'm overwhelmed by all she did for me. Anita didn't just remind me of sunshine—she is God's Son-shine in my life.

As a little girl, I held her picture in my hand. I never could have imagined that God would one day allow her to mentor me in real life. He alone could write that story. And although I may never fully understand how He weaves these moments together, I know this: He was directing our steps. And He takes pleasure and delight in doing the same for you.

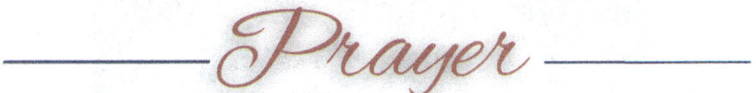

Lord, thank You for ordering my steps and taking pleasure in my journey. Even when the path is unclear, I trust that You are guiding me. Help me walk with confidence, knowing You are not only leading me—but delighting in me as I follow You.

In Jesus' Name, Amen.

How can you use your influence, big or small, to reflect the kind of love and encouragement that points others to Jesus?

Lesson 3
PEOPLE'S REJECTION BRINGS GOD'S REDIRECTION

At Texas Stadium walking up to my first DCC audition on April 3, 1993.

"In their hearts humans plan their course, but the Lord establishes their steps."
Proverbs 16:9

They called me "the comeback girl."

You see, I didn't become a Dallas Cowboys Cheerleader the first time I auditioned in 1993 at age 18. Or the second time in 1994 at age 19. After two crushing "no's," I came back five years later—at age 24—and finally made the team.

My journey to becoming a DCC was anything but easy. It was long, hard-fought, and transformative on every level. By the time I made it, I had invested every ounce of myself into preparing—mind, body, and spirit—for as long as I could remember.

It started as a childhood dream, but by my teenage years, it had become a lifestyle. My days revolved around dance classes, drill team, workouts, weight training, running, dieting, and trying every beauty treatment I could get my hands on. I even trained one-on-one with a recently retired DCC. I was all in.

As the date for my first audition approached, I drove two hours each way—on school nights—to attend DCC prep classes at Cowboys headquarters. Those classes were expensive and filled up fast, but I never missed an opportunity to be there.

To me, they were 24 karat gold. These classes offered a glimpse into the world I longed to be a part of. Taught by current DCC leaders and choreographers, they gave us insider tips and techniques—and a chance to be noticed by the legendary Director, Kelli Finglass, and prestigious Choreographer, Judy Trammell.

At my very first prep class, I was a starry-eyed 17-year-old kid, as nervous as a cat. I had memorized the faces of every DCC on my poster, so stepping into their studio and seeing them in person was rather intimidating. They were even more beautiful, more confident, and more dazzling than I had imagined.

One veteran stood out with her dynamic personality, commanding presence, and larger-than-life charisma. She owned the room. In contrast, while I could execute the choreography, I lacked that overflowing confidence—that "it factor" that separates a skilled dancer from an unforgettable performer.

Looking back, I understand now why I didn't make the team at 18 or 19. I needed more experience. More maturity. More showmanship. I had the desire, but I wasn't ready. God knew that.

He knew I needed time to grow—not just as a performer, but as a person. I lacked confidence, yet ironically, I also needed to learn humility. And most of all, I wasn't prepared for the mental toughness that the role of a DCC demands. But at the time, all I could feel was bitter disappointment. Rejection. Heartbreak.

What I didn't realize then was that people's rejection was part of God's redirection. He was leading me. Even through the "no's." Especially through the "no's."

If you're facing rejection right now, I want to gently ask: Will you surrender to Him? His plans are better than anything we could dream up on our own. You can trust Him. I promise.

Lord, thank You that when I feel rejected by people, You always accept me with unconditional love. What looks like a closed door is often Your hand, lovingly redirecting me. Help me trust that every "no" is part of Your greater "yes." Direct my steps, align my heart with Yours, and lead me on the path You've prepared.

In Jesus' Name, Amen.

Where in your life have you faced rejection or disappointment, and how might God be using it to redirect you toward His greater purpose?

Lesson 4
GOD LOVES US BECAUSE HE JUST DOES

My hometown was rooting for me, and I wanted to give them a victory more than anything.

"And I am convinced that nothing can ever separate us from God's love. Neither death nor life, neither angels nor demons, neither our fears for today nor our worries about tomorrow—not even the powers of hell can separate us from God's love. No power in the sky above or in the earth below—indeed, nothing in all creation will ever be able to separate us from the love of God that is revealed in Christ Jesus our Lord."

Romans 8:38–39

We really do learn the most through our trials. As the old saying goes: "No pain, no gain."

My years of not making the team were agonizing, but as I reflect on the details of that time, I can see how God used every aspect for my spiritual gain.

The day before my first DCC audition, I could hardly contain my excitement. It was my 18th birthday, and I had just become eligible—making the cut by the skin of my teeth. I was overflowing with hope and expectation, believing with all my heart for the best possible outcome.

The three-week audition process pushed me to perform beyond what I thought I was capable of. I made it to the final round, but when I walked out of Texas Stadium, I was crushed. I sobbed until I was physically sick. Years of dreaming, preparing, and striving ended in defeat. I felt lost and overwhelmed with sadness.

High school graduation came and went in a blur. I left home for Texas Christian University and joined the Delta Gamma sorority. Some of my sisters encouraged me to try out for the TCU Showgirls dance team, and thankfully, I made it. That "win" pushed me to keep going.

Then came round two.

One year later, DCC auditions rolled around again. I was terrified to put myself out there, but I couldn't shake the dream. I had a little more experience and maturity under my belt, and I was comforted by the fact that two of my friends would be trying out with me. But to my dismay, I was cut in the second round of the semi-finals. And my two friends? They made the team. I was happy for them—but it also felt like a slap in the face. I was mortified. Ashamed. Convinced I was a total failure.

The dream that had fueled me for so long suddenly felt foolish and out of reach. I had believed—deep in my heart—that this was meant to be. How could I have been so wrong? I was heartsick. I didn't want to show my face to anyone.

One of the hardest parts was feeling like I had let down my hometown of Sulphur Springs, Texas. The support had been incredible—local newspaper articles, church prayers, flowers, cards, and encouragement from people I didn't even know. They had believed in me, and I felt like I'd failed them all. On top of that, I knew there were people who wanted me to fail... and facing them was humiliating.

For a long time, I felt completely worthless and unlovable. I believed my value depended on what I could do, how I looked, and who I could please. I didn't understand that love—especially God's love—wasn't something I had to earn.

At the time, I didn't have a close relationship with God. Not like I do now. I thought I had to win His approval, just like I tried to win everyone else's. Consequently, achieving my dream was my #1 priority. At its core, I was striving to be worthy of love—while the One who already loved me unconditionally was right there waiting.

What I desperately needed to learn was this: God loves me... because He just does. And that's exactly what He began to show me in that season—and over the years that followed. While I was living out what felt like my worst nightmare of rejection, God was quietly, powerfully pursuing me. He was drawing me in—not because I succeeded or failed, but because I was His.

Why would God love us so passionately? Because He wants to. That's who He is. He is love.

And here's what I know now:
- Deserving His love is not a factor.
- Messing up is not a factor.
- People's rejection is not a factor.
- Our achievements—or lack thereof—are not factors.

None of these things can change His love for you and me. It doesn't have to make sense—it's love beyond our comprehension.

If we'll simply receive it with open hands and grateful hearts, God will help us let go of everything we're holding against ourselves. Jesus died on the cross for us—and that alone is more than enough. When we believe that truth and put Him first, we can live in the freedom of His grace and unconditional love.

That's what Romans 8 promises us:

> "Nothing can separate us from the love of God in Christ Jesus."

Looking back, I'm grateful I didn't make the team the first or second time. If I had, I might have missed the chance to learn what I needed most: God's love is constant, unshakeable, and not based on what I do—but on who He is.

He used my heartbreak to redirect me. And He will do the same for you. Because He loves us. He just does.

> **WHY WOULD GOD LOVE US SO PASSIONATELY? BECAUSE HE WANTS TO. THAT'S WHO HE IS. HE IS LOVE.**

Lord, thank You for loving me—just because You do. Not because of what I've done or haven't done, but simply because I'm Yours. Remind me daily that nothing can separate me from Your love— not fear, failure, or even my doubts. Your love is constant, perfect, and forever.

In Jesus' Name, Amen.

How has rejection or failure shaped the way you view yourself? How does God's unchanging love speak into that hurt today?

Lesson 5
WHAT GOD OPENS NO ONE CAN SHUT, AND WHAT HE SHUTS NO ONE CAN OPEN

My parents with me in Branson, MO after my show at Echo Hollow Amphitheater.

"Trust in the Lord with all your heart and lean not on your own understanding; in all your ways acknowledge Him, and He will guide and direct your paths."
Proverbs 3:5-6

In His amazing love and mercy, God gently picked me up and carried me through a new door. When I was at my lowest, He lifted me with His unconditional love. He relentlessly sought after me, and my heart began to understand how good He truly is.

At the end of my freshman year of college, my family and I traveled to Branson, Missouri—the live entertainment capital of America—to see our friend Debbie Money perform at one of the most popular venues: The Echo Hollow Amphitheater in Silver Dollar City. Not only was Debbie fantastic in the show, but to my complete surprise, she had an opportunity waiting for me. There was an open singer/dancer position, and she quickly connected me with the producer of the show. He asked if I could audition the very next morning. My heart raced between shock, excitement, and anxiety. I believe it was my parents' prayers that gave me the strength to say, "yes."

Mom and I made a late-night trip to the local Walmart to find something I could dance in, because I hadn't brought any performance clothes or shoes with me. I was completely unprepared for this sudden turn of events. Branson was 400 miles from home, and I had planned to return to college, but there I was.

God had opened a door—as only He could.

Early the next morning, I showed up for the audition. The show's dance captain taught me a fast-paced jazz combination. Next, I sang Elvis Presley's version of "Peace in the Valley" a cappella, since I had no accompaniment music! They asked me a few questions about my experience (which wasn't much), and I shared that I had been a finalist for the Dallas Cowboys Cheerleaders, which intrigued them.

When the audition was over, my family and I drove home feeling good about the whole ordeal. We were grateful, but with no expectations. Two days later, I got the call: "How soon can you move to Branson?" And before I knew it, I was performing at The Opera House and at The Echo Hollow Amphitheater, sharing the stage with my friend Debbie!

I was amazed.

And yet, I had perfect peace about stepping into this new adventure. Branson was beautiful, with a culture that valued God, family, and country. I was even introduced to a sweet Christian lady who needed a roommate—and I moved right in. It was clear that God had orchestrated every detail.

I relished the opportunity of entertaining for a living. Singing and dancing in Branson became my training ground in the performing arts. I had the privilege of working alongside seasoned professionals, skilled in every aspect of live theater. We performed multiple shows a day, six days a week—and during peak season, seven days a week.

I experienced every kind of onstage mishap you can imagine: I fell flat on my booty, had a coughing attack, broke a dress strap mid-song, was heckled, forgot lyrics, got a bloody nose, had a microphone die in the middle of a solo, was hit in the face with someone else's microphone, got stung by a wasp, slammed my hand in a truck door, and even had moments of laughter or emotion that I couldn't shake off. Through it all, I learned the show must go on. It was the best training I could have ever asked for.

Over the next five years, God knocked my socks off and continued to open doors for me. I worked in several other incredible venues with amazing people: The Shoji Tabuchi Theater, The Showboat Branson Belle, The Country Tonite Theater, and at The Will Rogers Theater.

I also had the joy of performing for a season in Pigeon Forge, Tennessee, at Dolly Parton's Music Mansion—an unforgettable highlight that included getting to meet Miss Dolly herself!

With Dolly Parton during my time in Pigeon Forge, TN.

One of the sweetest moments was when my hometown dance teacher, Durann Ardis, came to see me perform. She had always believed I could work in show business and encouraged me never to give up. When I saw her in the audience, tears filled my eyes. I was overwhelmed with gratitude for how faithful and good my Heavenly Father had been to me.

He had shut the door to DCC—for a season—and opened a door to something completely different. A place where I could grow not just as a performer, but as His child. When I had felt utterly rejected, God held me close and lifted up my head.

And in His infinite goodness, after my tenure as a DCC, He led me back to Branson, where I spent seven beautiful years performing at The Baldknobbers Theater. Every step of the way—without a doubt —God was the One opening and closing doors in His perfect timing.

Lord, You are the One who opens doors no one can shut. Help me trust You with all my heart and not lean on my own understanding. I surrender my plans to You and believe that Your way is always best.

In Jesus' Name, Amen.

Where might God be inviting you to step through a new door—even if it feels unexpected or uncomfortable? What's holding you back from saying yes?

Lesson 6
THE TRUTH WILL SET YOU FREE

Like sheep, we wander–but Jesus, our Good Shepherd, will always lead us back to truth and freedom.

> *"You will know the truth, and the truth will set you free."*
> John 8:32

Every day is full of choices. Some days we choose wisely; other days, not so much. We can know what's right yet still choose what's wrong. We can genuinely want to do good yet still fall into what's bad. That's why the Bible compares us to sheep and reminds us that Jesus is our Good Shepherd—He pursues us, rescues us, and brings us safely home into His care.

When the Lord opened the door to a new life in Branson, I couldn't deny His love. He didn't see me as a throwaway or a failure. He welcomed me as His daughter. Deep down, I knew that was the truth. And yet... I still gave ear to the enemy's lies. I still clung to shame.

Branson offered me a chance at a fresh start. But almost immediately, I found myself tangled in a mistake. During my very first audition interview, I shared that I'd once been a finalist for the Dallas Cowboys Cheerleaders. By the time I arrived to begin my new job, that detail had already spread through the grapevine. And unfortunately, the story had morphed—so not long after I started, I was faced with the terrifying question: "What was it like to be a DCC?"

I was caught off guard... and I froze. I didn't correct them. They were excited, and I desperately wanted it to be true. I made a choice at that moment... and I made the wrong one.

Out of pride, fear of rejection, and shame, I let the misunderstanding continue. That decision quickly became a heavy burden. But the shame I carried from my past—especially regarding the disappointment I'd caused people in my hometown—was something I didn't want to face again with a whole new set of people. So, I hid it. But now I was living under a new kind of shame: being dishonest.

Here's what I've realized: Shame grows in the dark but breaks in the light; and when it breaks, healing begins.

Over time, God gently led me to bring the darkness into the light. My soul had been tortured by the weight of the secret, but I feared that coming clean would be even worse. That's exactly how the enemy works—he convinces us that confession will crush us, when in reality, it frees us. The truth really does set us free.

Eventually, I repented of the lie. And I began to understand that the root of it wasn't just fear or shame—it was pride. I used to think pride only meant thinking too highly of yourself. I've since learned that pride can also show up as self-focus, even in the form of insecurity or self-loathing.

> **SHAME GROWS IN THE DARK BUT BREAKS IN THE LIGHT; AND WHEN IT BREAKS, HEALING BEGINS.**

I once heard, "Humility isn't thinking less of yourself—it's thinking of yourself less." That was a game-changer.

You can only imagine the overwhelming grace I felt five years later... when I actually made the DCC team. Looking back, I shake my head in wonder. God didn't leave me in my pit; He lovingly brought me out. He helped me face my shame with honesty and courage. And then He forgave me, redeemed me, and restored me.

I may have felt rejected by people, but God wrapped me in love. He didn't just clean up my mess—He called me to walk as a child of light, not shame.

Here's what I've learned to do when I mess up:

Confess it quickly.
Seek forgiveness.
Make it right.

Don't let shame fester in the dark.

I've also realized that when I carry shame, I'm not as gracious with others. But when I surrender my pride and bring things into the light, I experience God's forgiveness—and suddenly, I'm able to extend that same grace to others. That is freedom!

Lord, thank You for the truth that sets us free. In a world full of confusion and lies, help me cling to what is real and eternal. Shine Your light into every hidden place in my heart and set me free from fear, shame, pride and doubt. Your truth is my anchor, my freedom, and my guide.

In Jesus' Name, Amen.

Is there an area of your life where you've been hiding something out of fear, shame, or pride? What would it look like to bring that into God's light and let Him set you free?

Lesson 7
GOD'S MERCY IS NEW EVERY MORNING

DCC staff sent the alumni their original application packets as a keepsake. I was thrilled to look back on the memories!

"Because of the Lord's great love, we are not consumed, for His compassions never fail. They are new every morning; great is Your faithfulness."

Lamentations 3:22-23

In 1999, I felt ready to try again. Ready to pursue my dream of becoming one of "America's Sweethearts."

Back in the good ol' '90s, the process started with an old-school application—handwritten, of course. We had to submit an essay, photographs, and I even slipped in a CD of a few songs I'd recorded (they had singers in their show group, so it couldn't hurt, right?).

Then came the waiting game—several weeks to (hopefully) receive an approval letter by snail mail. If you were approved, you could show up for preliminaries.

I'll never forget walking into Texas Stadium that day with a peace that surpassed all understanding. I hadn't told a single soul I was auditioning again. If I made it: amazing. If I didn't, I was content with the beautiful life God had already given me, performing in Branson. Either way, I was in His hands.

Alongside hundreds of other eager women, I pinned my audition number to my bright pink leotard and joined the excitement—the kind you could feel in the air and smell in the hairspray cloud surrounding us!

Preliminaries were actually a blast. In groups of six, we introduced ourselves to the judges, then freestyled for three straight minutes to whatever music the DJ played. We all brought our best dance moves, high kicks, turns—even the occasional gymnastic feat—in hopes of catching the judges' eyes.

At the end of the day, the numbers of those advancing to the semi-finals were posted for everyone to see. The scene was a chaotic swirl of emotions—tears of joy, cries of disappointment. Out of over 600 ladies, about 100 of us were moving on to the next round... the very next day.

The semi-finals were much more intense. We learned a DCC-style dance—big energy, big smiles—and a tough high-kick routine. It was a test of who could pick up choreography quickly and perform under pressure. We even had to demonstrate right and left splits... ouch! If you could do all that and look like you were having fun, you had a shot.

We waited for hours as the judges deliberated. And strangely enough, instead of being filled with fear or anxiety, I found myself reflecting on just how faithful God had already been. I had peace. So, when the moment came to see the results, I knew whatever happened, I would be okay.

And then, the waiting was over.

I had made it to the finals!

I stood there in awe, taking it all in. Holy smokes... It was happening!

Then reality hit... I had just two weeks to prepare: choreograph a standout solo (complete with a killer costume and props to make it unforgettable), rehearse the two routines I had just learned, brush up on current events and football knowledge for the written test, and gear up for my interview with Director Kelli Finglass. Finals would be fierce—with 45 new finalists and a strong group of returning veterans all vying for the same coveted spots. (Yes, even DCC veterans have to re-audition every year!)

But through it all, one truth stood out: God is the God of second (and third... and tenth) chances.

All throughout Scripture, we see God rewriting stories that looked finished. He turns ashes into beauty, mourning into dancing, and brokenness into strength. His mercy doesn't run out—it renews. Every single morning.

In His hands, our past mistakes become testimonies. Our detours become divine direction. He faithfully restores the hearts that seek Him. He never gives up on us.

Prayer

Lord, thank You that Your mercy is new every morning. No matter what yesterday held, today begins with Your grace. Wash away my mistakes, renew my heart, and help me walk in the freedom of Your forgiveness. I don't deserve it, but You give it freely—and for that, I am deeply grateful.

In Jesus' Name, Amen.

Reflection

What lies has the enemy been whispering to you about your worth, your past, or your identity? How can you replace those lies with the truth that God's mercies are new every morning?

Lesson 8
COMPARISON DOES NOT DEFINE YOU

Every sunset is different, yet each one is beautiful... just like people, each unique in their own way, each one a masterpiece of God.

> "Make a careful exploration of who you are and the work you have been given, and then sink yourself into that. Don't be impressed with yourself. Don't compare yourself with others. Each of you must take responsibility for doing the creative best you can with your own life."
>
> Galatians 6:4-5 (MSG)

Being at the 1999 finals for the Dallas Cowboys Cheerleaders was a test of trust—trust in God's plans for my life. I didn't know if the dream I had chased for years was about to come true, ushering me into a whole new world... or if it was about to come to a definitive end. My heart pounded—not just from nerves, but from the weight of everything that had led to this moment. Whether I made the team or not, I knew this would be one of the most impactful moments of my life.

You could feel the energy in the room—each girl laser-focused, polished, and ready to leave it all on the floor. I remember sitting among the sea of hopefuls, grouped by how we looked. All the petite blondes with blue eyes (like me) were seated together. The tall brunettes were in another row. The redheads in theirs. It was like being lined up by categories, and I don't think I've ever been more visibly compared to other human beings than I was during those DCC finalist experiences.

And that's the truth—comparison was part of the process. The judges had to evaluate, contrast, and choose who they believed best fit the team. That's just how it works. But let's be honest—no one likes being compared to others.

Even today, I don't love it when I compare myself to others—or when others compare me to someone else. Comparison can rob us of joy and the sense of purpose God has uniquely given each of us.

I may have looked like five other girls in that audition room, but God had a very specific plan for me. And He has one for you. See, we've got to learn to separate the world's rankings and evaluations from our true worth. God never uses comparison as a tool to measure our value—or to determine our calling. He calls us each by name.

So when those comparison thoughts creep in—and they will—we have to recognize them for what they are: the enemy's way of distracting and discouraging us from walking confidently in the lane God marked out just for us.

GOD NEVER USES COMPARISON AS A TOOL TO MEASURE OUR VALUE.

Instead, we take those thoughts captive. We speak truth over them. We remind our hearts that we are each uniquely created by God, and any thought that tries to steal our joy, peace, or confidence has no place in our minds.

God has too many incredible things for us to do to waste time on comparison!

Ephesians 2:10 reminds us:

"For we are God's workmanship, created in Christ Jesus to do good works, which God prepared in advance for us to do."

Whether you're currently in a season of comparison, have been there before, or will face it in the future—remember this: your worth is not measured against anyone else. The world may compare, but your Heavenly Father never does. You are already chosen, already loved, and already enough in Him.

Lord, help me to celebrate others without diminishing myself. When comparison creeps in, replace it with gratitude. Help me see myself through Your eyes—deeply loved, created in Your image, and called for a purpose. Let my heart rest in the truth that I am already enough in You.

In Jesus' Name, Amen.

What lie about your value or calling do you tend to believe when you compare yourself to others? What truth from Scripture can silence that lie?

Lesson 9
WITH GOD, ALL THINGS ARE POSSIBLE

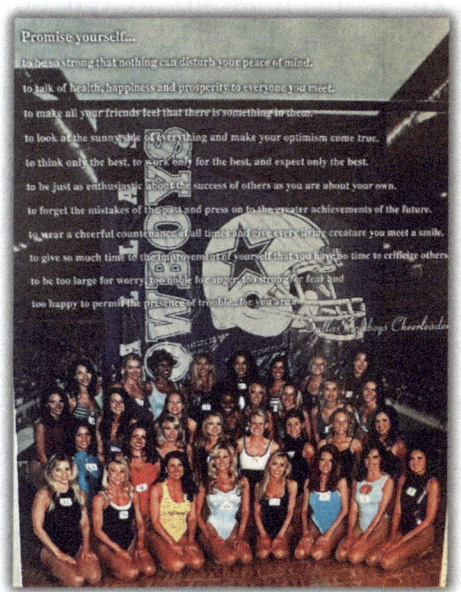

1999 DCC Training Camp Candidates!

"Jesus looked at them and said, 'With man this is impossible, but with God all things are possible.'"

Matthew 19:26

On paper, it didn't make sense for me to come back and audition again—and it certainly didn't make sense for me to actually make the team. I had already built a new life in Missouri, with a home, a career, and a path that made sense. But sometimes, logic takes a backseat to the dreams that never let go of your heart.

There are moments when your soul holds its breath—and deep

inside you dare to believe, "What if?"

So there I was, standing in that audition room once again, waiting to hear my fate. I had already heard "no" twice before. Same dream. Same room. Some of the very same judges. Truthfully, the odds didn't look great. I knew what it felt like to walk out with a forced smile and a heavy heart. But I also knew what it felt like to get back up again, fueled by a fire that had never burned out.

By the third audition, I had done everything I could do. I trained harder. I prayed more. I matured—not just as a performer, but as a woman learning to surrender her dreams to God's hands. I truly meant it when I said, "Lord, if it's not Your will, I trust You." That kind of surrender doesn't come easily. But it comes when you've been humbled by disappointment and carried by grace.

When the judges re-entered the room and the DJ started playing "If My Friends Could See Me Now," the classic DCC theme song, chills shot through me. After hours of debating and decision-making, they were finally ready to announce the results. I braced myself for anything. And then, I heard it. My name. I was officially going to training camp!

Time stood still. My breath caught. Tears immediately welled up, not just from excitement, but from the overwhelming awareness that this was God's doing. He had carried me through the "no's," refined me through the waiting, and now He was allowing me to step into a long-awaited "yes."

It wasn't just about making the team. I had learned that when we trust God with our dreams—even when it hurts, even when it feels impossible—He is always working. And when He opens a door, no one can close it.

If you're in a season of waiting or facing what looks like another closed door—don't lose hope. Keep showing up. Keep preparing. Keep praying. Because the same God who moved mountains in my life is working in yours. His timing is perfect. His plan is good. And with Him, all things truly are possible.

Lord, thank You for placing dreams in my heart and for walking with me through every step—especially the hard ones. Help me to surrender the outcome to You and trust that Your ways are higher than mine. Strengthen my heart while I wait, and remind me that with You, nothing is impossible.

In Jesus' Name, Amen.

What dream or desire in your life feels impossible right now? How can you surrender it fully to God while still believing He can make a way?

Lesson 10
TRUE PEACE IS TRUSTING THAT GOD IS IN CONTROL

The One who gave it all invites me to fix my eyes on Him and live in His peace.

"Do not be anxious about anything, but in everything, by prayer and petition, with thanksgiving, present your requests to God. And the peace of God, which transcends all understanding, will guard your hearts and minds in Christ Jesus."

Philippians 4:6-7

When I was in training camp, I was thrilled to be so close to making the team, but in all transparency, the pressure was *intense*. The enormity of the NFL stage, the high expectations of the Dallas Cowboys Cheerleaders organization, and the professionalism of the returning veterans completely unnerved me. I'd look around and think, "This can't be real. Do I even have what it takes to be here?"

Behind the scenes, I was a mess of nerves. Sleepless nights, anxious dreams, a constant pit in my stomach—I felt anything but peaceful. The fear of failure was real. Even though I was deeply grateful to be there, I felt like I was living on the complete opposite side of peace.

For the first time, my dream was becoming a reality—and that made me feel incredibly vulnerable. I had tasted it, and now I knew exactly what I stood to lose. But walking forward in faith, even while fear tried to paralyze me, taught me something powerful: True peace is trusting that God is in control, despite how I'm feeling in the moment.

So when my mind was racing and my body was full of stress, I held onto one truth: God is sovereign. The enemy was loud, my flesh was weak, but my spirit was anchored in Him. I knew He had brought me here, and that deep, unshakeable trust in His plan—that was real peace. The kind that doesn't always feel calm but carries you through anyway.

When I think about Jesus in the Garden of Gethsemane, preparing for the cross ahead, I'm reminded that even He experienced deep emotional and physical stress. He sweated drops of blood. His body responded to the weight of what was coming. And yet, He was at peace, because He fully trusted His Father. Jesus knew He was fulfilling the plan. That's what peace looks like—it transcends all understanding. It's rooted in complete surrender.

> *"Fix your eyes on Jesus, the pioneer and perfecter of faith. For the joy set before Him, He endured the cross, scorning its shame, and sat down at the right hand of the throne of God." – Hebrews 12:2*

I've learned when your body is reacting in fear and the enemy is pressing in, don't confuse that chaos with a lack of peace. Keep praying. Keep praising. Keep pressing into God.

Peace isn't always a feeling—it's a decision to trust.

And when you choose to trust Him, God will show up strong. He'll work in you and through you in ways that go far beyond what you could do on your own. With Him, you can do it afraid... and still walk in true peace.

Lord, help me not to be anxious but to bring everything to You in prayer with a heart full of thankfulness. I know that true peace comes when I trust that You are in control. Calm my heart, guard my mind, and fill me with the peace that only You can give—a peace that goes beyond understanding.

In Jesus' Name, Amen.

What does it mean for you personally to "fix your eyes on Jesus" in the middle of stress or uncertainty?

Lesson 11
WHEN IT'S ALL ABOUT ME, HAPPINESS WILL FLEE

The Bible, coffee, and my curious pup. Focusing on Jesus... gives me joy and strength.

"The joy of the Lord is your strength."

Nehemiah 8:10

Every time I walked into practice at Cowboys Headquarters in Valley Ranch, I was motivated by the giant inscription that stretched across the dance studio wall. I still think about it to this day:

"Promise yourself to be so strong that nothing can disturb your peace of mind.

To talk health, happiness, and prosperity to every person you meet.

To make all your friends feel that there is something in them.

To look at the sunny side of everything and make your optimism come true.

To think only the best, to work only for the best, and to expect only the best.

To be just as enthusiastic about the success of others as you are about your own.

To forget the mistakes of the past and press on to the greater achievements of the future.

To wear a cheerful countenance at all times and give every living creature you meet a smile.

To give so much time to the improvement of yourself that you have no time to criticize others.

To be too large for worry, too noble for anger, too strong for fear and too happy to permit the presence of trouble."

I truly feel my best when I approach life with this type of positive, gracious, and purpose-driven attitude. But I feel my worst when my thoughts turn inward: dwelling on how so-and-so shouldn't have spoken to me that way... or thinking someone should've done that differently... or wishing I had this and looked like that... or wondering if things will *ever* get better... or believing I'll never be enough. You get the idea!

I've learned that a self-centered life is a miserable life. God gave me a little saying that I remind myself of often: "When it's all about me... happiness will flee!"

When I start spiraling downward emotionally, it's usually because I'm too focused on me. Sure, something difficult may have happened or someone may have irritated me—but the real issue is often what I'm choosing to concentrate on. That's when it's time to shift my focus back to Jesus. He heals our hearts and our thinking. We can ask Him, "Lord, how do You want to use me for Your purposes today?"

The joy of the Lord really is our strength. He has lifted me up again and again, helping me redirect my thoughts and realign my perspective with His. When we fix our eyes on Him, everything begins to shift. His joy gives us the strength to keep going AND to bless the people around us!

Lord, You are my joy and my strength. When I feel weak, remind me that Your joy lifts me and carries me through. It's not about me or my circumstances—it's all about You. Direct my heart and mind to fulfill Your purposes today.

In Jesus' Name, Amen.

What's one practical way you can live out the saying, "When it's all about me... happiness will flee"?

Lesson 12

WAITING ON THE LORD IS WORTH IT

DCC Team Bonding Event at Southfork Ranch.

"Let us not grow weary in doing good, for at the proper time we will reap a harvest if we do not give up."

Galatians 6:9

The journey through Dallas Cowboys Cheerleader training camp stretched every part of me—physically, mentally, emotionally, and spiritually. Each day demanded more grit, more grace, and more growth than the one before. There were complex routines to master, critiques to take with humility, and uniform fittings that reminded us just how closely we were being evaluated. And always lingering in the air was the possibility of hearing your name called— for a cut.

It was high pressure. High stakes. And sometimes, low spirits. But God was there—in the long, exhausting rehearsals, in the whispered prayers under my breath, and in the quiet car rides home where I often wrestled with doubt.

He met me in the middle of my uncertainty and reminded me that perseverance isn't about being perfect. It's about showing up when you want to quit and trusting Him to carry you the rest of the way.

Every drop of sweat, every sore muscle, every tear that fell during late-night prayers—it was all part of the refining process. I didn't always feel strong, but I kept going because He was strengthening me. I wasn't just being prepared for a team... I was being transformed by His presence.

And then came Southfork Ranch.

Our team bonding event was exactly what I didn't know I needed—a weekend of laughter, fresh air, and connection in the same iconic setting where the TV series *Dallas* was filmed. I secretly kept hoping J.R. and Sue Ellen Ewing would appear and join us by that famous pool!

But even more meaningful than the scenery was what happened around the dinner table. We shared stories, laughter, fears, and dreams. The women around me weren't just teammates—we were becoming sisters. Being there for one another through all the highs and lows was building something lasting—a bond like family: strong, rooted, and united.

And then came one of the most magical moments of my life: the squad photo reveal. I can still feel that moment—standing shoulder to shoulder with the women I had cried, prayed, and fought beside... watching as our faces appeared on that iconic poster.

We had made it. Not just onto the team, but through the process. Through the pruning. Through the pressure.

It was joy and disbelief all at once. I had known the sting of rejection, the pain of almosts, and the ache of waiting. And yet, deep in my spirit, I had never stopped believing. Even in seasons of defeat, something in me held on—because I knew if God wanted it for me, He would make a way.

Making the team wasn't just a personal victory—it was a sacred confirmation that God had been building something far more meaningful all along: a deeper trust in His timing, a steadier walk in His grace, and a stronger belief in His love.

Because when you wait on the Lord, He really does make it worth it.

> **EVEN IN SEASONS OF DEFEAT, SOMETHING IN ME HELD ON— BECAUSE I KNEW IF GOD WANTED IT FOR ME, HE WOULD MAKE A WAY.**

Prayer

Lord, thank You for being with me every step of the way—for carrying me when I felt too weak to continue. Thank You for showing me that waiting seasons are not wasted seasons. Help me to trust Your timing, even when it's hard, and to remember that every trial holds the potential for transformation. Turn my waiting into worship and my trials into testimony.

In Jesus' Name, Amen.

Reflection

What does it look like for you to turn your "waiting" into worship and your "trial" into testimony?

Lesson 13
PREPARATION TODAY IS WHAT YOU'LL BE THANKFUL FOR TOMORROW

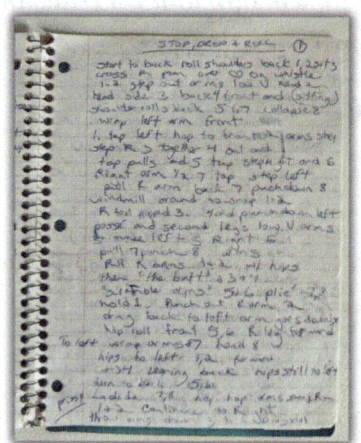

Before digital downloads and iPhone video cameras, we wrote down our choreography and tape-recorded the music from rehearsals at the DCC studio!

"Ponder and meditate on (the Scriptures) day and night, making sure you practice everything written in it. Then you'll get where you're going; then you'll succeed."

Joshua 1:8

For me, one of the toughest tests of being a Dallas Cowboys Cheerleader was the sheer amount of preparation required. Let me elaborate. We were responsible for learning over 50 Texas Stadium-worthy sideline dances! Our squad also had to execute choreography for the pregame show, the players' entrance, the fight song, the 2-minute warning dances, and the big halftime productions. Every time we performed on the gridiron, things got especially complicated. Each of us had exact yard lines to get to for every formation change—no guessing, no winging it.

Rehearsals were long and intense. We practiced in the dance studio on weeknights, then spent hours upon hours rehearsing at the stadium before each game. The expectations were clear: If a cheerleader missed one rehearsal before a home game, she couldn't perform at that game. If she missed two, she would be released from the squad.

And then there was the traveling show group—an entirely different level of commitment altogether. We had separate rehearsals for dance and vocal numbers, not to mention the lightning-fast costume, accessory, and prop changes. We traveled to 11 different countries and all across the States. I wish I knew how many places we prepared special performances for... we even danced on a small carpet laid out on an ice hockey rink! It was so much fun, but I'm getting tired just thinking about it!

Memorizing the choreography was big—but even bigger was mastering showmanship, power, and "hairography!" Yes, flipping our hair on specific counts was actually choreographed. Our Director, Kelli Finglass, reminded us that our dancing had to be dynamic enough to capture the attention of the fans sitting all the way up in the nosebleeds of Texas Stadium.

No matter how naturally gifted or talented someone was, none of this could be pulled off without a gargantuan amount of preparation. From our very first meeting, we understood that making the team meant going above and beyond. We were called to strive for excellence, pay attention to the smallest details, go the extra mile and make a special effort to do more. And honestly? We were thrilled to do it!

When I cheered, there were no iPhones, no easy music downloads, and no apps to organize choreography. We came to practice with old-school jam boxes, ready to record the music straight from the speakers. Then we'd write hundreds of dance sequences and diagrams into spiral notebooks. That was the only way to keep up with the massive amount of material we needed to learn. And we practiced at home and on work breaks... anywhere, anytime... any chance we got.

If the Dallas Cowboys Cheerleaders didn't take preparation seriously, they wouldn't be where they are today. It takes a crazy amount of work to make it look easy. And the same is true in our walk with Christ.

How we prepare in private shows up in public.

Take David, for example. Before he faced Goliath, he defeated the lion and the bear—when no one was watching. His private victory prepared him for his public one.

When we prepare for our day by spending time in God's Word and in prayer, we carry His wisdom and His strength into everything we face. The preparation may be quiet and unseen, but the fruit is resonant and undeniable. Preparation today is what we'll be so thankful for tomorrow. Today's discipline truly leads to tomorrow's blessing.

Lord, help me plant seeds of discipline, learning, and faithfulness today so that I may walk in wisdom tomorrow. Teach me to value small steps and quiet growth, knowing You are shaping my future through my choices now. Lead me with Your truth, and give me the patience to trust Your process through preparation.

In Jesus' Name, Amen.

Think about David's story of fighting the lion and the bear before facing Goliath. What "lions and bears" might God be using in your life right now to strengthen your faith for what's next?

Lesson 14
GOD BRINGS PURPOSE FROM PAIN

Taking a water break during practice at Texas Stadium.

"The Lord disciplines those He loves, as a father the son He delights in."

Proverbs 3:12

When I look back on my time training as a Dallas Cowboys Cheerleader, I can almost feel the burn in my hip flexors. You see, high kicks that weren't so high were a deal breaker. We had to be able to get those kicks up, up, up! My best strategy was to wear ankle weights to practice. The goal? Build strength and muscle memory so that when it was time to perform—without the weights—my legs would practically fly up and smack me in the face.

And honestly, that image has stuck with me ever since. It reminds me that strenuous training makes the real deal a joy to do.

It's the same with life. Looking back on the harder seasons—times I felt stretched, overwhelmed, or just plain exhausted—I now realize that God used it all to train me. He was building endurance in me, refining my heart, and teaching me to lean into Him when I had nothing left. That extra pressure? That opposition? It had a purpose. He used all of it to prepare me—to make me stronger for better days ahead.

The tricky part, of course, is that when we're in the middle of the pain, we usually don't recognize it as potential preparation. We just want it to stop. But God, in His grace, doesn't waste anything. He will use it all.

Years after leaving the field, I faced struggles I never could've rehearsed for: seasons of disappointment, heartbreak, unexpected detours, and hard goodbyes. And yet, I could feel that same spiritual "muscle memory" kicking in. Every single time God had been faithful before, and the strength He'd built in the quiet—rose up in me when I needed it most.

If you're walking through a season of struggle, testing, or opposition right now, I want to encourage you that God will use it to prepare you for something you can't yet see. He will develop you for His purposes, just like He did with people in the Bible—Joseph in prison, Esther in the palace, Ruth in the fields, and David in the pasture.

We're always growing—always becoming. But the harvest will come. So, keep worshipping. Keep praying. Keep showing up in His Word. When the time is right, those "weights" will be removed, and your testimony will soar higher than you ever imagined! Your pain is not pointless. There is purpose in it. And your story is still being written.

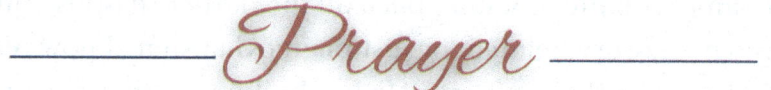

Prayer

Lord, thank You for loving me enough to correct and shape me. When pain comes, help me trust that You always bring purpose from every tear. Teach me to see Your hand in my training, and to appreciate that You discipline those You delight in. Strengthen my faith and remind me that no season is wasted in Your hands.

In Jesus' Name, Amen.

Reflection

What spiritual "muscle memory" has God developed in you—truths or habits that help you endure when new trials arise?

Lesson 15
GOD SEES YOUR POTENTIAL

Reuniting with our amazing coach, Judy Trammell, head choreographer for the DCC.

"I will put them into the fire; I will refine them like silver, and test them like gold. They will call on My Name and I will answer them; I will say, 'They are my people, and they will say, 'The Lord is our God.'"

Zechariah 13:9

A great coach doesn't just see where you are—they see who you can become. They'll turn up the heat and push you past what you thought was possible. I still remember our choreographer and coach, Judy Trammell, expressing that if she wasn't calling us out, it meant she had given up on us. Her message was clear: The hard critiques came because she believed in us.

At the time, being called out was tough—honestly, I felt the fire many times! But looking back, I think: "Yes! God used her coaching to sharpen my skills, shape my character, and grow me from the inside out."

She had a way of refining base metal into 24-karat gold.

But let's be real: When you're in the fire, it's uncomfortable. Sometimes I just want to wave the white flag and say, "Lord, can't I just stay here in what's familiar and easy?"

But God, the ultimate Coach, sees something in us we can't always see in ourselves. And because He loves us, He refuses to leave us where we are. He never gives up. Ever!

I want to encourage you that if God is "calling you out," it's because He sees incredible potential in you. He loves you passionately and relentlessly... enough to call you up higher.

And just like a good coach, He balances it all perfectly. He celebrates progress, honors obedience, rewards perseverance, and invites us into holy rest. He knows when to push and when to restore. You can trust Him in both the fire and the stillness.

The fire may feel fierce, but so is God's love for you. You can be sure... everything He does... makes you better.

> "For You, God, tested us; You refined us like silver... but You brought us out to a place of abundance."
> - Psalm 66:10-12

Lord, refine me in Your holy fire—burn away what doesn't belong and shape me for Your purpose. But in the heat, remind me of Your goodness. Let Your blessing anchor me and Your rest renew me. Teach me to trust both the flame and the stillness, knowing You are in them both.

In Jesus' Name, Amen.

Do you feel the "fire" in any area of your life right now? Can you see that God is turning your "base metal into 24 karat gold"?

Lesson 16
GOD HAS A DEEPER PURPOSE FOR YOU THAN MEETS THE EYE

A dream realized.

"And who knows but that you have come to your position for such a time as this?"

Esther 4:14

I remember thinking, "If I can make it to the first game, I'll finally believe I'm an official Dallas Cowboys Cheerleader!"

So when that first game came, you'd think it would've felt like I'd reached my end goal. But it didn't. It absolutely felt like just the start. I could sense that God had so much more to show me—so much more to teach me—than I ever expected. The Lord had me there for a reason I was only beginning to understand.

I looked around at the incredible women beside me, each of us dressed in the iconic blue and white. Then I glanced down at my polished white cowboy boots, the rhinestone-encrusted stars on my white shorts, the silky blue blouse tied in a knot, the fringed vest with more of those sparkling stars, and the glittering pom-poms in my hands... gulp... it felt like an out-of-body experience.

My dream had taken me on a roller coaster ride to get here, but there was no doubt in my heart—God had planted that dream long before I understood the "why."

Even in the middle of all the excitement, I could feel something deeper stirring. This wasn't just about dancing, performing, achieving, or winning. It was about bringing joy. Inspiring others. Representing something bigger than ourselves.

Esther is one of my favorite heroines in the Bible. Scripture tells us she had a deeper purpose than what could meet the eye. She was exactly where God wanted her to be. She made an incredible impact, "for such a time as this." I believe each of us can look at our own lives and circumstances and hear those same words spoken over us.

We sometimes think that living with purpose means standing on a stage, preaching from a pulpit, or traveling across the world to serve. But the truth is—God places us exactly where we're meant to be. Whether it's a football field, an office, a classroom, or a living room—He will work through us for His glory.

> **GOD SEES THE WHOLE PICTURE. HE'S DOING SOMETHING DEEPER WITH YOUR LIFE—RIGHT HERE, RIGHT NOW.**

That first game taught me that being a DCC was so much more than just checking off a personal dream. God had made me an overcomer. He had brought me so far. And I came to know—I was called to that role not just to perform, but for Him to work through me.

He had given me an unbelievable opportunity to encourage others... to love and serve people I would never have met on my own... and to share my faith more widely than I ever imagined.

You may not fully understand why you're in the place you are right now, but trust this: God sees the whole picture. He's doing something deeper with your life—right here, right now.

Lord, thank You for placing me exactly where I need to be. Help me to see Your deeper purposes. Let me represent You in every space I step into, and remind me that I am here for such a time as this.

In Jesus' Name, Amen.

How can you invite God to work through the ordinary spaces of your life—your job, home, friendships, or community—for His glory?

Lesson 17
GOD BLESSES UNITY

Laughing with each other as we traveled the world created beautiful unity.

"I urge you to live a life worthy of the calling you have received. Be completely humble and gentle; be patient, bearing with one another in love. Make every effort to keep the unity of the Spirit through the bond of peace."

Ephesians 4:1-3

The wow factor of every DCC stadium performance is a crazy stunt we like to call the "jump splits!" If you're unfamiliar with this feat, let me explain. We would link up in a kick line, simultaneously jump up, do the splits in the air, and then dramatically land in those splits... on the cold, hard ground!

You could always hear the crowd gasp in surprise... every single time!

Besides the dire need for flexibility, the key to the jump splits is unity. It's about caring for your teammates' well-being. You must be mindful of those around you and stay in sync with your team as a whole. If you are not, someone can seriously get hurt.

To do the jump splits, you connect arm-in-arm and support one another, yet you absolutely cannot put any pressure on your neighbor. You must keep your core tight, maintain good posture, and pull your own weight. You have to be strong independently, and then you become *exponentially stronger* when you link arms.

Practicing together for hours upon hours was no joke. We had to have a team mindset and function as a synchronized unit... or else it was gonna end in a big ol' disaster!

Fun fact: During the high kicks and jump splits (at every Cowboys game), we were cheering one another on at the top of our lungs:

"You got this!"
"Let's go DCC!"
"Almost there!"
"You can do it!"

It took every ounce of stamina we had to cover that massive field in an energetic pregame show—finishing with a marathon of kicks and an exclamation point of the jump splits.

Cheering for one another made our job of cheering for the Cowboys... a success. Working together to accomplish results... way greater than we could ever do individually... was invigorating!

A mentor once told me, "One snowflake on its own melts quickly, but when many come together, they can stop traffic."

It's exactly the same way in the body of Christ, the church. When each of us pulls our own weight, yet links arms in support of one another... watch out, world! God commands the blessing where there is unity, and when brothers and sisters get along. (See Psalm 133.)

The world is pretty brutal, and if we don't have each other's backs, there's no hope for us to make a true and lasting impact of love and light in the darkness. It's not easy to execute the jump splits, and it's even more difficult to stay in unity as the church, but we have to be willing to put in the work!

Being unified and cheering for one another will make our job of cheering for God (worshipping Him in everything we do) a blessing beyond our imaginations.

Lord, thank You for the gift of unity. Help us to walk in humility, patience, and love as we support one another. May Your Spirit guide us in peace, and may our unity bring You glory.

In Jesus' Name, Amen.

Who has God placed beside you to "link arms" with in this season? How can you intentionally cheer them on and strengthen your unity?

Lesson 18
ALWAYS KEEP YOUR EYES ON JESUS

A treasured gift from my friend Sarah Melton–her artwork captures my journey of worship and is a reminder to keep my eyes on Jesus.

"I keep my eyes always on the Lord."
Psalm 16:8

At Dallas Cowboys games, we never knew what "stadium jam" the DJ would play next. He was a master at playing the perfect music at the perfect time to go with the flow of the game, and we had to be ready to follow suit. This made our time on the sidelines nerve-racking—but also exciting!

Two things had to happen: dedication to knowing 50+ dances,

and dedication to following our group leader.

I realized very quickly that following my leader—who was a five-year veteran and knew things I simply couldn't know—was the only way to survive and ultimately succeed. The sidelines were tricky, with tons of media and people vying for their piece of Cowboys Nation (not to mention humongous football players who could come barreling toward us at breakneck speed and force). It was easy to get distracted.

Believe it or not, the DJ would sometimes play random songs that weren't in our choreography repertoire. So, our group leader had to call out the name of a routine instantly, and we would follow her lead... doing our best to make it work. The goal was: "Never let 'em see you sweat!" You see, our director and choreographer were watching carefully. They were taking notes, and if we didn't perform up to standard, we could be cut from the next game or even cut from the team. Honestly, I think my brain got more of a workout during the games than my body!

Focusing on and following my leader was a great lesson in how to flourish under pressure and how to be an effective team player. This lesson is important in NFL games... but more important... in everyday life.

In this crazy life, two things have to happen: dedication to knowing the 66 books of the Bible, and dedication to following our leader, Jesus.

Just like the hectic sidelines of Texas Stadium, life can distract us with overabundant media, people vying for their place in the world, potentially dangerous threats, and unexpected "music" that is totally out of our control.

But when we daily study God's Word—His "choreography" and His ways—we will build a strong foundation of His truth and wisdom to draw from. And when we focus on our leader, Jesus, by praying, worshipping and following His lead—obeying His voice and imitating His actions—we will flourish under pressure and be an effective team player. We can trust Him! He knows things we simply couldn't know.

We can look to wise leaders further ahead in their journey... but always, always, always keep our eyes on Jesus—our perfect leader—the One who will never leave us or forsake us. He is the only way to our survival, and ultimately our success in everything that matters.

Lord, help me to keep my eyes focused on You. When distractions come, draw my heart back to Your truth. In every high and low, may I look to You for strength, guidance, and peace. You are my constant, my Savior, and my hope.

In Jesus' Name, Amen.

What's one area of your life where God might be calling you to trust Him even when the plan—or the "song"—changes unexpectedly?

Lesson 19
DOING THINGS GOD'S WAY TAKES DETERMINATION

*Nourishment for my mind, body and spirit:
the Word, water, sun butter, and a green apple.*

"Now to Him who is able to do immeasurably more than all we ask or imagine, according to His power that is at work within us, to Him be glory in the church and in Christ Jesus throughout all generations, forever and ever! Amen."

Ephesians 3:20-21

A friend once asked me, "If walking closely with Jesus brings so much joy, peace, love, and wisdom... then why doesn't everyone do it?" Great question. The first thing that came to mind was something I learned during my DCC days: If I started my day with healthy food and conditioning, I had more energy, stamina, and strength to perform at my very best. That discipline carried me through long rehearsals, endless kick lines, and four-hour game days under the Texas sun. And yet—many times I obliterated healthy habits that fueled me best.

So why don't we just do what we know will bring the best outcome? As I thought about it, the Lord brought a list of "D" words to mind—reasons we often drift away from walking closely with Him: Distraction. Deception. Defiance. Discouragement. Detours. Distrust.

In Acts 4, we see how walking in step with the Holy Spirit results in a powerful life—one that makes a difference and brings glory to God. But the opposition is fierce. Much like a high-pressure audition or a grueling practice, the pressure is real—we'll face pushback from the enemy and from the world. And that leaves us with a decision: Will we give in—or will we be determined to trust God and keep walking with Him?

Because the results are worth it. But the journey requires: Determination. Discipline. Dedication. Direction. Diligence. Dependence.

I remember learning new choreography that seemed impossible at first. My muscles burned, my timing was off, and I doubted if I could ever master it. But step by step, repetition by repetition, determination carried me through. And then one night—under the stadium lights—I realized God had given me the strength to do what once felt overwhelming.

It's the same in faith. The decision to trust and obey God can feel so difficult in the moment. But when I take that step of obedience—He takes over. He strengthens me. And I know it's Him doing the real work.

I've come to call this the "Hard-Easy" path. It's hard at first, but so much easier in the long run. The alternative? "Easy-Hard." Doing what feels easy now... but paying for it later in difficulty, regret, or spiritual distance.

James 4:6–8 says:

> "God opposes the proud but gives grace to the humble. Submit yourselves, then, to God. Resist the devil, and he will flee from you. Come near to God and He will come near to you."

Just like the father of the prodigal son, God is waiting with open arms. Submitting to Him isn't something to fear—it's actually a relief.

I used to believe the lie that fully submitting to God would be stifling. But I've discovered the opposite is true. Walking with Him is a delight. Just spending time with Him daily—in His Word and in prayer—brings joy, peace, love, and wisdom. He meets us in our hardest moments, strengthens our steps, and never fails us.

So let's be determined to do things God's way. Don't miss out on the joy of knowing Him, serving Him, and loving Him—whether under stadium lights or in the everyday moments of life.

> **GOD IS WAITING WITH OPEN ARMS. SUBMITTING TO HIM ISN'T SOMETHING TO FEAR— IT'S ACTUALLY A RELIEF.**

Prayer

Lord, following Your way isn't always easy, but it is always best. Give me the strength and determination to choose Your path, even when it's hard. Help me stay faithful, focused, and bold in obedience. Thank You for the amazing joy of walking with You!

In Jesus' Name, Amen.

Reflection

What's one area of your life where God is calling you to choose the "hard-easy" path—doing what's difficult now but leads to long-term peace and joy?

Lesson 20
BE A STUDENT OF THOSE AROUND YOU

Both award winning, Richard Gere (actor) and Robert Altman (director) visited DCC rehearsal to prepare for the movie, "Dr. T. and the Women."

"Blessed is the one who finds wisdom, and the one who gets understanding."

Proverbs 3:13

We were drilling routines (per usual) at the DCC dance studio when—believe it or not—Richard Gere casually strolled through the door! We all gasped, giggled, and clapped like little kids. He looked exactly like he did in *Pretty Woman*, just dressed down in a ball cap, glasses, T-shirt, and jeans. His movie *Runaway Bride* had just come out, so talking to him face-to-face felt totally surreal.

He wanted to meet us because... we were going to be in his next movie!

The film was *Dr. T. and the Women*, directed by Robert Altman. The storyline was set in Dallas, and Richard Gere played a wealthy doctor surrounded by high-maintenance women. Ha! One of those women—his daughter—was trying out for the Dallas Cowboys Cheerleaders. That's where we came in. Our job was to surround her and just act like... us!

Mr. Gere was very kind and unpretentious. He asked a ton of questions and seemed genuinely interested in our DCC world. He mingled with us for a few hours and even asked me, "So what do you think about filming a movie? Have you done any acting before?"

I have no idea what I said to the man. I was too starstruck to form a level-headed answer!

A few weeks later, it was time to film—and we were thrilled to find out we'd be working with Kate Hudson, who played the role of "Dr. T.'s daughter." We spent the entire day with her, from sunup to sundown, filming two short scenes that required endless takes and dance repeats. We were used to practicing nonstop, but that day we did the same routine what felt like forty times in a row!

During a lunch break, I ended up at Kate Hudson's table. She was refreshingly down-to-earth and super friendly—despite being Hollywood royalty (her parents are Goldie Hawn and Kurt Russell). She asked us all kinds of questions about our dance backgrounds, what DCC auditions were like, and how it felt to perform at Texas Stadium.

It struck me that these two major stars were the ones asking us questions. I know it was part of their process to prepare for their roles, but it left an impression on me. They taught me something I'll never forget: When someone asks thoughtful questions and truly listens, it makes you feel seen, heard, and valued.

That experience helped me realize how much we can learn from the people around us—when we take the time to ask, observe, and seek understanding. Everyone has something to teach if we're willing to be students.

If I could go back, I'd ask so many more questions. I may not be surrounded by movie stars today, but I am surrounded by super stars for Jesus—every single day. I'm thankful that I can gain so much insight and perspective from others... simply by watching and asking. AND it's beautiful to see someone light up when you take an interest in their story.

It's a blessing to learn from the people God places in our lives. Every person is truly a priceless treasure. As Scripture reminds us:

> **"Do nothing out of selfish ambition or vain conceit. Rather, in humility, value others above yourselves."**
> **- Philippians 2:3**

P.S. Dr. T. and the Women wasn't exactly a box office hit... but it sure was fun to be a part of it!

Lord, thank You for the people You've placed in my path. Give me a humble heart to learn from them, to listen well, and to grow in wisdom. Help me recognize the lessons You're teaching me through others.

In Jesus' Name, Amen.

Philippians 2:3 reminds us to value others above ourselves. What's one practical way you can show someone today that their story and experience matter to you?

Lesson 21
DEDICATE EVERYTHING YOU DO TO THE LORD

On our USO tour to Korea, visiting with children of military personnel, we ended up being more blessed than the kiddos.

"Whatever you do, work at it with all your heart, as working for the Lord, not for human masters, since you know that you will receive an inheritance from the Lord as a reward. It is the Lord Christ you are serving."

Colossians 3:23-24

When people find out I was a Dallas Cowboys Cheerleader, one of the first questions they often ask is: "How much did you get paid?"

I always smile a little before I answer. Back in 1999–2000, we earned $50 per game. If you were chosen for a special appearance, you might make $250 to $500, depending on the event and your seniority. Our uniforms were provided, along with hair and nail upkeep and travel expenses for out-of-town events.

Rehearsals weren't paid back then—though that's changed in recent years. Today's DCCs are compensated for those hours, which I think is absolutely wonderful. And in 2025, they received a 400% raise—which I celebrate wholeheartedly!

Growing up in the '80s and '90s, I witnessed the Dallas Cowboys in their heyday, and the cheerleaders as their ambassadors across God's green earth. I saw the DCCs on TV, in magazines, and on posters all over Texas. In the dance world I lived in, they were icons. So, when I dared to dream of becoming a DCC, I knew it would mean stepping into something so much bigger than I could even imagine—something that came with unique experiences and opportunities I couldn't find anywhere else.

It was a different era—and right or wrong, I simply never saw being a DCC as a job. It was my dream. From the beginning, I understood we were required to either have a full-time job or be a full-time student, and I knew exactly what the compensation was. I was completely willing to work long hours, endure the physical grind, push through the mental pressure, and make the demanding schedule work. Honestly—I would've done it for free!

And here's the lesson I learned in the process: When we give our best with a sincere heart, God blesses us in ways we can't always measure. He shapes our character, deepens our faith, multiplies our joy and prepares us for what's next.

I've seen this to be true—not just as a DCC, but in every job and every ministry I've served in. I certainly don't always get it right, but when we offer our efforts to God, the ordinary becomes sacred. Even the smallest tasks take on eternal purpose when they're done for Him.

That doesn't mean we shouldn't advocate for fair pay or value ourselves professionally—absolutely we should. But at the end of the day, the lesson I keep coming back to is this: Whatever you do, do it for the Lord.

He's the One we're really serving. And when we give Him our best, He always uses it for something greater.

Lord, help me dedicate every effort, every job, every act of service to You. Remind me that I'm not working for recognition, but for Your glory. Let my heart stay focused on You, and let my life reflect that You are worthy of my very best.

In Jesus' Name, Amen.

How would your definition of success change if you measured it by fruitfulness rather than income or outcome?

Lesson 22
BE CONCERNED WITH WHAT CONCERNS GOD

Our next stop was to visit soldiers at the DMZ in Korea. Smiles, hugs, and our attentive listening meant the most to our military heroes there.

> "The Lord does not look at the things people look at. People look at the outward appearance, but the Lord looks at the heart."
>
> I Samuel 16:7

I'll be honest—during my DCC journey, I became overly concerned with my appearance. What began as discipline and self care, soon slipped into an obsession with chasing an image that I could never quite obtain.

There's nothing wrong with wanting to look your best, present yourself well, or enjoy style and beauty. These can all be good things. But it's easy to place too much value on them.

What makes a great DCC isn't just a cultivated look. It's the heart behind the uniform—the perseverance that doesn't quit, the giving spirit that serves in the community, the dedication to the sisterhood of the team, and the way you share love and light to others. Outward image may get people's attention, but it's the condition of your heart that captures God's.

That truth reminded me of a sociology experiment I once participated in during college. A few of my classmates were assigned by the professor to dress in drastically different outfits. Then our entire class loaded up in our cars and headed to the shopping mall. We were instructed to nonchalantly observe how store clerks treated the differently dressed "student shoppers." One wore expensive, trendy clothes with perfectly groomed hair and makeup. Another dressed in simple jeans and a t-shirt. A third sported a dramatic, unusual style—combat boots, spiked hair, and a silky kimono. The last dressed in old, dirty, worn-out clothes.

The results were eye-opening. The student in high-end fashion was treated like royalty. The one in average clothes was treated averagely. The one dressed unusually got attention, but mostly negative. And the one in shabby clothes? Ignored, dismissed, or treated rudely. Sadly, with no exceptions.

That experiment stuck with me. It was such a clear picture of how quickly we are to size people up based on appearance—and how it can affect the way we treat them.

James 2:1–4, 8–9 puts it plainly:

"My brothers and sisters, believers in our glorious Lord Jesus Christ must not show favoritism. Suppose a man comes into your meeting wearing a gold ring and fine clothes, and a poor man in filthy old clothes also comes in. If you show special attention to the man wearing fine clothes and say, 'Here's a good seat for you,' but say to the poor man, 'You stand there,' or 'Sit on the floor by my feet,' have you not discriminated among yourselves and become judges with evil thoughts? ... If you really keep the royal law found in Scripture, 'Love your neighbor as yourself,' you are doing right. But if you show favoritism, you sin..."

The world has always placed a huge emphasis on image—and it probably always will. And yes, it's good to take care of ourselves. But God reminds us in His Word that what matters most is our heart. He isn't fooled by the surface. He isn't impressed with appearances. He's looking deeper, into the place that reveals our truest selves.

As a DCC, I saw firsthand how people often judged the uniform before they ever knew the girl wearing it. But behind every uniform—and behind every face in the crowd—there's a heart God treasures.

Today, let's commit to reflecting God's heart in all we do—caring for others and ourselves with grace. Instead of obsessing over our outward appearance, let's remember that what matters most is the heart. And may we treat everyone with the kindness and respect that come from seeing people the way He sees them.

Lord, help me care most about what matters to You. Teach me to value what You value and see beyond appearances. While the world looks at the outside, You look at the heart—help me to do the same. Keep me from being overly concerned with image, and let my life reflect Your heart above all.

In Jesus' Name, Amen.

How can you intentionally see people the way God sees them this week— beyond appearances and assumptions?

Lesson 23
KINDNESS IS KEY

Hanging onto my hero, my sister, Kathryn Clifton Jones.

> "Put on then, as God's chosen ones, holy and beloved, compassionate hearts, kindness, humility, meekness, and patience."
>
> Colossians 3:12

I can always count on my big sister, Kathryn, to have my back. During my time as a Dallas Cowboys Cheerleader, she was juggling a lot—married, raising two young kids, and teaching school—yet somehow, she still managed to be my breath of fresh air when I was barely keeping my head above water. She gently redirected my heart to what matters most.

Sometimes all it took was a phone call or a handwritten note from her—small, simple things that brought me such unexpected kindness, I would be overwhelmed with joy and gratitude. And you know what? Her acts of kindness made me want to pass them on. Kindness has a way of creating a beautiful ripple effect.

One of the kindest gifts she ever gave me was simply being a safe place. I could show up as I was—flawed, weary, and messy—and she just loved me anyway. No expectations. No pressure. Just grace.

When you're a performer, people often see you as a product instead of a person. Their expectation is to be entertained, so acknowledging your struggles or humanity just kind of ruins their fun. I get it. But every person—on every stage and in every seat—needs someone they can be real with. We all need that one person who doesn't care about what you can produce, but just cares about you.

This may sound like a simple, feel-good message—but don't dismiss it. Kindness is powerful. It matters to God. In fact, He calls us to clothe ourselves in it.

> **HER ACTS OF KINDNESS MADE ME WANT TO PASS THEM ON. KINDNESS HAS A WAY OF CREATING A BEAUTIFUL RIPPLE EFFECT.**

When we prioritize kindness, it changes the atmosphere of our lives. It can soften hearts, shift relationships, and even restore hope. And the most amazing part? God multiplies it in ways we may never see or fully understand.

When I received sincere kindness from my sister, God used it to breathe life into me. I know firsthand how deeply needed it is in this world. It's not just a suggestion—it's a requirement from the heart of God:

"He has told you, O man, what is good; and what does the Lord require of you but to do justice, and to love kindness, and to walk humbly with your God?"
- Micah 6:8

Lord, thank You for the gift of kindness. Remind me that even the smallest act, when done in love, can carry great power. Help me reflect Your heart through gentle words and compassionate actions. Let kindness flow from me as a testimony of Your grace.

In Jesus' Name, Amen.

Who in your life has shown you unexpected kindness that deeply impacted you? How can you extend that same kindness to someone else this week, creating a ripple of your own?

Lesson 24
BE GRACIOUS, YOU DON'T KNOW WHAT PEOPLE MAY BE FACING

It was an honor to meet Shania Twain!

> "Live out this God-created identity the way our Father lives toward us, generously and graciously, even when we're at our worst. Our Father is kind; you be kind."
>
> Luke 6:36 (MSG)

One of the best parts of being a DCC was getting to work with so many amazing people. We were blessed to meet Shania Twain at the height of her career. She was the best-selling female country artist of all time and truly a mega star. Her songs, "You're Still the One," "Man! I Feel Like a Woman!" and "From This Moment On," were basically the soundtrack of my life back then. She was filming a TV special at Texas Stadium to air after the 1999 Thanksgiving Cowboys game, and I was beyond excited to be part of it and to meet *THE* Shania Twain!

I remember being in awe of her fame, beauty, and talent. But what intrigued me most was how quiet she was. I expected her to be super-outgoing and to dominate the room, but she was actually quite shy. She seemed like her thoughts were a million miles away. However, when it was showtime, she was in her element. She lit up the stage for the thousands gathered to see her and beautifully sang all of her hit songs.

Years later, I read her autobiography and was stunned by her story. She had endured so much—poverty, hunger, abuse, and the tragic loss of both parents in a car accident when she was just a teenager. And at the time I met her, she was going through unimaginable heartbreak. Her husband had just betrayed her by having an affair with her best friend, leaving her and their young son behind.

All of that was happening behind the scenes while the world saw a flawless, glamorous superstar. I never would have guessed what she was truly going through based on appearances. It was such a powerful reminder: We never know what someone is carrying.

Grace matters. We need to show it freely and generously, just like God does for us. No matter who we're talking to—a celebrity, a stranger, or someone in our own home—we're called to love with His love. Some people are tough, yes (you know the ones), but God still asks us to be kind, because only He truly knows what's going on in their hearts.

We're not called to judge. We're called to love. We all need grace... we all need forgiveness... we all need the cross. To quote Shania's beautiful lyrics:

"Let every man help his brother/Hallelujah, hallelujah
Let us all love one another"

Prayer

Lord, help me to extend grace to others, even when I don't understand their actions. Remind me that every person is carrying burdens I cannot see. Teach me to love with the same grace and generosity You show me every day.

In Jesus' Name, Amen.

Reflection

Who in your life right now could use an extra measure of grace, patience, or understanding from you?

Lesson 25
GOD WANTS TO WORK THROUGH ALL OF US

The legendary Deion Sanders.

"You are Christ's body—that's who you are! You must never forget this. Only as you accept your part of that body does your "part" mean anything."

1 Corinthians 12:31 (MSG)

The electric personality of Deion Sanders will be seared in my memory forever. It was close to Thanksgiving 1999 when I arrived at Children's Medical Center in Dallas for one of the most impactful experiences of my life. Three other DCCs and I were given the honor of accompanying Deion to bring love and care to the patients and their families that day.

I remember being so nervous walking through the doors of the children's hospital—not just because I was about to meet Deion

Sanders, but because I didn't know what I could possibly say to families facing such heartbreaking circumstances. But the moment I saw Deion—jersey on, full-length fur coat, sparkling bling, amazing shades, and the biggest smile you can imagine—I knew it was going to be a phenomenal day!

I loved watching the kids and their families light up when they saw Deion. He brought the same passion to the hospital that he showed week after week on the football field. With his signature "Prime Time" energy and genuine care, he made every child feel special. I was so grateful to play even a small part in bringing joy to those families that day. Deion was the star, but even in my supporting role, I could contribute too.

God can use our favorite football stories or just about anything we are willing to share... to bring love and cheer to those who need it.

Whenever we walk into a room, we'll find people who are starving for kindness, care, and love. And the truth is, we don't have to be a star to make a difference—God can use any of us to bring hope. He longs to shine His love and light through each one of us. Even the smallest expression of love can leave an eternal impact. We'll never regret saying, "Yes, Lord. Here I am. Send me!"

Deion Sanders may be one of the most gifted athletes of our time, but his greatest legacy is how intentionally he cares for people. That's the true playbook we can all follow.

Lord, thank You for creating me with purpose and for reminding me that I am part of Christ's body—that's who I am. Teach me to embrace the part You've given me, knowing my life has meaning when I accept it. Use me to bless others and to reflect Your light, serving with joy, love, and a willing heart.

In Jesus' Name, Amen.

What does saying, "Yes, Lord. Here I am. Send me," look like in your current season of life?

Lesson 26

GOD WORKS ALL THINGS FOR GOOD FOR THOSE WHO LOVE HIM

My beloved, Jerod.

"And we know that in all things God works for the good of those who love Him, who have been called according to His purpose!"

Romans 8:28

I met my husband, Jerod, just before I became a DCC. His mom actually set us up on a blind date, and we instantly hit it off. But Jerod was very cautious from the start. I still remember him telling me, "I can't have a girlfriend right now—I need to stay focused on graduate school and can't afford any distractions."

Challenge accepted!

I knew in my heart that he was the one. I absolutely loved everything about him... but I wasn't about to let him know that! Ha!

A few months after we met, I was selected to go on a USO tour to Europe with the Dallas Cowboys Cheerleaders Show Group. On the flight to Budapest, I became seriously ill. After landing, I saw a doctor who discovered my white blood cell count was dangerously high—he suspected appendicitis.

I was heavyhearted. I felt like I was letting my team down and was so disappointed not to be able to perform for our amazing U.S. Military. All that hard work and preparation... gone. I was flown by emergency medical transport to Ramstein Air Force Base in Germany. I'll never forget how miserably sick I felt—and how scared I was, thousands of miles from anyone I knew. There's no doubt in my mind that the prayers of my mom, dad, sister, and Jerod carried me through that horrific experience.

While recovering in the hospital, I had a lot of time to think and pray. From my sickbed, I wrote out what I really wanted in life: to serve God and marry Jerod. I gave it to the Lord and put it in His hands. When I finally made it home, the very first thing that happened was... Jerod proposed!

It took all of that nonsense for him to come to his senses! But truly, every time something hard, scary, or painful happens, we can look back and see how God brought something good from it. In the moment, it's hard to understand. It's difficult to believe any good could come from the trial. That's why it's so important to look back and remember God's faithfulness.

In this case, He sent a soldier to pray over me during the care flight, a chaplain to counsel me in the hospital, He healed my body, re-centered my life priorities, strengthened me from the inside out... and yes, moved Jerod's heart too!

God is *always* working for our good.

Lord, thank You for the promise that all things work together for good for those who love You and are called according to Your purpose. When life feels uncertain, help me to rest in the truth of Your faithfulness. Remind me of all the ways You've carried me before, and let that assurance strengthen my trust today. I know You are working—even when I cannot see it. I place my hope in You.

In Jesus' Name, Amen.

When you look back on your life, what moments remind you that God was working for your good, even when you couldn't see it?

Lesson 27
HONOR THE ONES WHO SACRIFICE FOR YOU

The USO tours were life changing experiences, and I am forever grateful to our service men and women.

> "...the Son of Man did not come to be served, but to serve, and to give His life as a ransom for many."
>
> Matthew 20:28

Even though my first USO tour ended in pain and agony—with me laid up in the hospital—just five months later I experienced a sweet redemption. I was thanking God for second chances as our DCC show group traveled to Korea and Okinawa to spend Christmas with American soldiers stationed there.

It was an honor beyond anything I had hoped for or imagined. But it came at a cost: missing Christmas with my family for the first time in my life. That's when I began to understand just how much our military men and women give up year after year—holidays, birthdays, countless precious moments, and the comforts of home—to protect the rest of us back in the good ol' USA. My brief taste of their sacrifice left a lifelong impression.

For two weeks, we ate in mess halls and shared meaningful conversations with homesick soldiers. Every night we performed a full-fledged variety show at multiple bases. Our setlist included classic rock 'n' roll, country music, Christmas carols, and patriotic songs. One of my favorite moments was singing the Chicks' (formerly The Dixie Chicks) "I Can Love You Better" and choosing a soldier from the audience to dance with me. It was always a blast! And it never failed... when we sang "God Bless the USA," tears filled the eyes of so many who were far from home.

Many soldiers wrote us letters afterward, and we always wrote back. It was a mutual exchange of gratitude—reminders of home and heartfelt thanks for courage and sacrifice.

Traveling from base to base by helicopter or bare-bones plane added to the adventure. We sat along the walls, harnessed in—just like in the movies. One time, we had to make an emergency landing in a remote field, and let me tell you—my life flashed before my eyes more than once.

Yet the moment that marked me most happened on Christmas Eve. Around midnight, as we flew back to our home base, a soldier asked if we would sing "Silent Night." Over the roar of the helicopter, through our headsets, we sang together: *"Sleep in heavenly peace/sleep in heavenly peace..."*

As the last note faded, we all cried like babies. That Christmas—removed from our family, friends and homeland—brought the true meaning of the season into focus. The men and women willing to sacrifice everything, even their lives, so that we could live freely... pointed my heart straight to Jesus: He was born to save us.

"With the angels let us sing/Hallelujah to our King/Christ the Savior is born/Christ the Savior is born"

My time overseas was not only an unforgettable glimpse into the sacrifices made for our freedom—it was a powerful reminder of the ultimate sacrifice Jesus made to bring us eternal life. For both, I am deeply and forever grateful.

Lord, thank You for coming not to be served, but to serve, and to give Your life as a ransom for many. Today, I'm especially grateful for those who follow Your example—our military and so many others —who willingly sacrifice for the good of their fellow man. Bless and protect them, and help me never take their service or Your ultimate sacrifice for granted.

In Jesus' Name, Amen.

Jesus gave everything for you. What does it look like, practically, to live your life as a "thank You" to Him?

Lesson 28
TAKE TIME TO REMEMBER WHAT GOD HAS DONE

My sweet niece, Eretria, visiting the DCC locker room.

"Once again I'll go over what God has done, lay out on the table the ancient wonders; I'll ponder all the things You've accomplished, and give a long, loving look at Your acts."

Psalm 77:11-12 (MSG)

One Christmas, I experienced a full-circle moment that warmed my heart. My precious 8-year-old niece had the chance to cheer at the Dallas Cowboys' Stadium for a youth football event. While she toured the Cheerleaders' locker room, her mom sent me the sweetest text: They had found my ornament—made many years ago

—hanging on the DCC Christmas tree. With hundreds of ornaments on that tree, it was no easy find.

Every year, rookie DCCs create a Christmas ornament to celebrate their first season. These ornaments are passed down to inspire future DCCs. Mine is a tiny pink ballet costume on a little hanger with the words: "I have dreamed of becoming a DCC since I was a child in a pink tutu. This Christmas, I hope your dreams come true! Love, Carolyn Clifton."

Seeing that ornament through my niece's eyes reminded me how important it is to pause and celebrate the milestones in our lives—and to pass on encouragement and hope to the next generation. The DCC organization does this beautifully. Their traditions connect alumni, current cheerleaders, and future hopefuls in a chain of inspiration and faith.

Much like traditions, remembering God's faithfulness—regularly and intentionally—isn't just helpful; it's biblical. Holy Communion, Holy Days, and Holy Scripture are all ways God gently stirs our hearts in gratitude, reminding us of who He is and what He has done. And this remembering isn't only for us—it's for those who come after us, so they too may know His goodness.

> *"These commandments that I give you today are to be on your hearts. Impress them on your children. Talk about them when you sit at home and when you walk along the road, when you lie down and when you get up. Tie them as symbols on your hands and bind them on your foreheads. Write them on the doorframes of your houses and on your gates."*
> *- Deuteronomy 6:6–9*

We all suffer from a little spiritual amnesia now and then, so reminders are our friends! That tiny rookie ornament reminded me that God had strengthened me to never give up on my dream. I didn't become a DCC in my own strength—it was only by His grace. And the story doesn't end there. When my niece discovered that special keepsake, it encouraged her own dreams and taught her that God's faithfulness carries through generations. Truly, a full-circle moment... pointing to His goodness and provision.

Lord, I choose to remember the works You have done—to reflect on Your faithfulness and meditate on all Your mighty deeds. Thank You for the full-circle moments in my life that remind me You are always with me. Keep my heart open to pass on Your faith, hope, and love to the next generation, so they too may see and trust Your goodness.

In Jesus' Name, Amen.

What's one "ornament" in your life— a moment, memory, or keepsake – that reminds you of God's faithfulness?

Lesson 29
BOUNDARIES EXIST TO PROTECT YOU

Jerod and me at the Dallas Cowboys Christmas Party located in the Stadium Club at Texas Stadium.

"Submit yourselves to God. Resist the devil, and he will flee from you. Come near to God and He will come near to you."

James 4:7-8

One of the clearest boundaries for a Dallas Cowboys Cheerleader was this: no dating the players!

Back home, people would tease me, "I bet you'll be dating Troy Aikman in no time!" Those kinds of jokes always made me laugh, but I would set them straight: "Don't be talking crazy and starting rumors—you'll get me kicked off the squad!"

There's no doubt—maintaining professionalism was a healthy and necessary boundary within the organization.

On occasion, there was definitely flirting between players and cheerleaders, but I was with Jerod and had no interest in any trouble. So if anyone tried to hit on me, it was easy to shut it down. I'd mention my amazing man and make it crystal clear—with my words, tone, and body language: "Nope! Not an option." With a solid stance of "I am his, and he is mine," the guy would get the picture and vamoose!

Anytime the enemy comes around to tempt us, we can treat him the same way. We can maintain our boundary and take a firm stance, saying, "Nope! Not an option. I belong to Jesus. I'm His, and He's mine." And the devil has no choice but to flee. He knows he's beaten.

Satan is no match for God. Not even close. He's not God's opposite or equal—God's power is infinitely greater. Still, the enemy's goal is to take as many people down with him as he can. And even if he can't steal our salvation, he'll try to steal our joy, peace, and purpose.

Sometimes we don't even realize it, but we end up resisting God instead. For example, maybe we were rejected by someone we loved, and deep down, we still want to vindicate ourselves. Our pride keeps us from surrendering the hurt to God. We start looking to people for acceptance, approval, identity, and value—trying to make that wrong "right" in our own way, instead of trusting God to do it.

So, in a situation like someone trying to hit on us... if we're looking for validation from others, it can be tempting to entertain that attention.

Satan is sneaky, and most of the time, it's not a sudden fall—but a slow, step-by-step compromise that pulls us off course.

But when we submit to God, the Holy Spirit strengthens us to resist the bait. He gently reminds us that what looks tempting will only lead to harm, while God's way always leads to life.

That's why the fear of the Lord—the awe and reverence of who He is—is the beginning of wisdom (Proverbs 9:10). When we understand how loving, powerful, and good He is, submitting to Him becomes the safest and smartest thing we can do. He's the One who makes wrong things right. He's the One who heals and redeems. We don't have to fight battles on our own—He fights for us.

I believe that submitting to God and living within His boundaries spares us so much unnecessary heartache. But we also have to recognize that the enemy doesn't give up easily. He may not get us in one area, but he'll try another. Even Jesus—perfect and sinless—had to resist the devil. And what did He do? He quoted Scripture to the enemy. And so should we: "I submit to God, so you must flee in the Name of Jesus! I'm drawing near to God, and He is drawing near to me!"

Our mighty God will place a boundary around us and keep us secure and protected. He always gets the victory!

> **I BELONG TO JESUS. I'M HIS, AND HE'S MINE.**

Prayer

I submit myself to You, resisting the enemy and drawing near to Your presence. Help me to see that Your commands are not burdens, but gifts meant to protect and guide me. Cleanse my heart, steady my mind, and lead me in Your truth. Thank You for loving me enough to set boundaries that keep me close to You. Thank You for victory in You!

In Jesus' Name, Amen.

Reflection

Which Scripture could you begin declaring over your life when the enemy tries to tempt or discourage you?

Lesson 30
BE RESPECTFUL TOWARD THOSE WHO SEE THINGS DIFFERENTLY

Jerod and me: raw sienna and cotton candy pink.

> "But the wisdom that comes from heaven is first of all pure; then peace-loving, considerate, submissive, full of mercy and good fruit, impartial and sincere."
>
> James 3:17

No doubt, Dallas culture is glamorous and fashionable—with bold southern flair thrown in for good measure. They say everything is bigger in Texas, especially the hair! I grew up in this culture, where we didn't leave the house unless we were fully "dolled up." So it didn't surprise me that one of the rules of being a DCC was to always be presentable—even if we were just walking out to the mailbox.

We had a guidebook with beautiful pictures of veteran DCCs demonstrating what was appropriate to wear at a theme park, out to dinner, or through the airport. Dressing up and being as perfectly groomed as possible was required. We also attended etiquette classes to prepare for formal events. On some occasions, we were placed in the company of five-star generals, heads of state, and celebrities. We never knew from week to week what events, people, or circumstances were coming our way.

My husband, Jerod, was raised to live "off the land" and "off the grid" in Star Valley, Wyoming. When his family went camping, they wouldn't go to a campground with amenities. Nope—the further away from civilization, the better. On the other hand, I had never camped a day in my life until I met my hubby. For real—his background and mine are polar opposites. If we were crayons, he'd be "Raw Sienna," and I'd be "Cotton Candy Pink!"

Jerod loves tapping into his roots. With a true backwoodsman's spirit, he planned a weekend retreat for 20 family members in a remote (4-wheel-drive required) cabin. I'm talking about the booniest of the boondocks—no cell service! By the time we arrived, our truck was completely coated in mud. One family member had to abandon their little car because it got hopelessly stuck in the muck. As I surveyed the situation, I couldn't help but wonder, "What in the world was this husband of mine thinking?"

I could see Jerod was eating all this rustic adventure up with a (whittled-out-of-tree-bark) spoon. But I found myself rolling my eyes on more than one occasion. For instance, he and his brother literally cleared a "beach" for us on the river with a machete and chainsaw—killing a snake and two black widow spiders in the process!

Just when I was nanoseconds away from unleashing my critical opinion, this thought occurred to me: "Do I want him to succeed or not?"

Then a flood of questions rushed through my mind: "If he makes a few mistakes—or just does things differently than I would—can I give him grace? Am I going to jump at the opportunity to critique him, or can I support him? If I had planned this trip, how would I feel if he questioned and criticized my choices? Are we a team or not?"

Wow. I needed that internal "come to Jesus" meeting. I tend to forget that men deeply desire respect. R-E-S-P-E-C-T. So I bit my opinionated tongue and decided to act on what Ephesians 5:33 says about marriage:

> *"Let each one of you love his wife as himself, and let the wife see that she respects her husband."*

It felt really good to let my husband thrive in who he is—and to trust him. It turned out to be a fantastic weekend, full of adventure and memories! And I have to admit... by showing my husband respect, he was inspired to be more loving toward me. Respecting him and our differences opened up a floodgate of love. Since then, we've truly gained a better marriage.

It's funny to look back and realize how much I've mellowed since being a DCC. These days, you'll often find me with no makeup, in leggings and a big T-shirt, shopping at Walmart! And my husband has mellowed (big time), too. Learning to weigh our priorities on the scale of life—and finding balance together—has made loving and respecting one another awfully sweet.

Lord, fill me with Your wisdom that is pure, peace-loving, gentle, and full of mercy. Help me to treat others—especially those who think or live differently—with respect, patience, and grace. Let my words reflect Your love, and may peace be the fruit of my life.

In Jesus' Name, Amen.

In what ways can you show respect and trust toward the people God has placed in your life—especially when they do things differently than you would?

Lesson 31
MAKE LOVING DEPOSITS IN THE LIVES OF OTHERS

Our Director, Kelli Finglass, blessed us with her words of encouragement as she visited with us at a DCC Alumni Reunion.

"Praise be to the God and Father of our Lord Jesus Christ, the Father of compassion and the God of all comfort, who comforts us in all our troubles, so that we can comfort those in any trouble with the comfort we ourselves have received from God."

2 Corinthians 1:3-4

Through my experience as a DCC, I learned to balance critiques and praise. To this day, the significance of "making deposits" and "making withdrawals" has made all the difference in my relationships.

Can you relate to this scenario?

My husband walks into the room looking tired and frustrated.

His body language says, "Can I have your attention?" I'm settled into my favorite chair, with my favorite coffee, and a new project on my mind. I'm anxious to zone out on my Pinterest app. I have a choice: I can make a deposit or a withdrawal. I wish I could say that I always choose to do the right thing, but I can't!

However, here's what it looks like if I make a deposit... I put my phone down (because that stinkin' thing is *THE* most distracting object on the planet), and I sincerely listen—with everything I've got. I let him know that I truly believe in him. More importantly, I remind him: "If God is for you, who can be against you? I know you're going to overcome this battle because I've seen you do it time and time again."

The old and cheesy cheer comes up and out of the recesses of my brain: "Jerod, Jerod, he's the man! If he can't do it, no one can!" We laugh, and I give him a hug and kiss (probably all I needed to do in the first place). Even though I haven't solved his problems, making that deposit into his "account" helps him go from being in the red to back in black.

Here's another scenario...

A friend apologizes (for the hundredth time) for her messy car, house, and appearance. Her eyes say, "I'm failing."

I can make a deposit. One of the best things we can do is to see the beauty in someone—and then speak it. I tell her honestly, "When I see you, I see beauty. The mess that comes with kiddos, working, and serving is not important. What I do see is that you're investing in people's lives, and that is priceless. AND... you are incredibly beautiful."

Even if the world never acknowledges what she does in a day, it all matters to God. I see that she's storing up treasure in heaven. She is not failing; she's actually succeeding in the most important things.

Here's another…

My child is down. Peers and the inevitable pressures they bring are so draining. I can make a deposit. I take a "mental time-machine journey" back to how it felt to be in school. I try to see things from his young perspective… right where he is. I tell him sincerely, "I wouldn't change one thing about you."

Part of my job is to teach and correct, but my child needs to know—without a doubt—that I think he is perfectly created just the way he is. I hug him tightly and pray over him, asking God to fill him with strength and wisdom to resist peer pressure.

Here's another…

A custodian in the mall is doing her job, but she looks weary and dejected. I can make a deposit. I give her a warm, sincere smile. I look her in the eyes and ask, "How are you doing today?" Then I listen and offer her a word of encouragement. It's not much, but kind words, respect, and simple acknowledgement help raise her "account balance."

Again, I wish I could say this is how I always choose to act. But what if I'm the one who's bankrupt? You see, I'm often unable to make a deposit because I'm overdrawn myself. But dear friend…

We can receive a deposit. If you want to be rich, let your Father God deposit His love, grace, and truth into you!

When our account is full from God's deposits—when we spend time with Him in His Word, in prayer, in worship, in His presence—we have plenty to share with others. Then we can make deposits into others' accounts all day long, only to receive more into our own again the next morning when we seek Him.

You are worth His infinite deposits. Our God is so generous and will fill you to overflowing, allowing you to share His wealth with the people in your life.

Lord, thank You for comforting me in every trial so that I can comfort others with the same love You've shown me. Help me to be intentional in making deposits of kindness, encouragement, and grace in the hearts of those around me. Use my life to reflect Your love and bring hope wherever it's needed.

In Jesus' Name, Amen.

Who in your life could use a "deposit" of kindness, encouragement, or grace today—and how can you offer it?

Lesson 32
FOCUS ON THE REAL THINGS OF GOD

Walking my pups in God's beautiful creation helps me to refocus my heart on what is real and true.

"Finally, my friends, keep your minds on whatever is true, noble, right, pure, lovely, and admirable. Don't ever stop thinking about what is truly worthwhile and worthy of praise."

Philippians 4:8

Maybe you've watched the TV shows *Dallas Cowboys Cheerleaders: Making The Team* on CMT or *America's Sweethearts: Dallas Cowboys Cheerleaders* on Netflix. And maybe you're curious about whether these shows genuinely portray the reality of the DCC world.

I'd say yes... and no! These docuseries capture many real aspects of becoming a DCC. But a TV show can only offer a condensed representation of a multilayered, years-long, real-life journey. Most of the day-in, day-out reality would never make the cut. The entertaining highs and dramatic lows always take center stage.

Like you see on screen, the "highs" are full of once-in-a-lifetime moments: professional makeovers, being fitted for the iconic uniform, being named an official Dallas Cowboys Cheerleader, performing at electrifying Cowboys games, working with celebrities, traveling the world, and more. These experiences have been part of being a DCC—long before reality TV.

And the "lows" are real too: blunt critiques, painful injuries, and tearful cuts from the team—moments that stretch the candidates and push their limits physically, mentally, and emotionally. (Side note: It was even harsher back in the day!) Becoming a DCC is, without question, a catalyst for becoming tougher than nails— inside and out.

But despite the allure of highs and lows, the most important part of life happens when the cameras aren't rolling. When we are alone and completely real with God, He does His most profound work within us. That's where His truth cuts through the noise and shows us what is truly worthwhile.

God doesn't measure us by our highlight reels or lowlight moments. He sees who we are becoming in our daily walk with Him. He sees our hearts, our character, and the fruit of His Spirit in our lives. These are things the world might overlook but are priceless to Him.

Unlike the roller coaster stories and edited clips of most media, God never changes—He is the truest, most real foundation in the universe. So I encourage you to press into what is truly real: His Word and His Presence. When we choose to focus on the true and real things of God, we are putting Proverbs 4:23 into practice:

"Above all else, guard your heart, for everything you do flows from it."

We are filling our hearts with God's goodness and consciously guarding the world's untrue, ignoble, wrong, impure, unlovely, and unadmirable things from seeping in. We are becoming steady, secure, and grounded—and our actions will reflect His love.

In true reality, God sees you. He loves you. And He wants to be with you in it all—your highs, your lows, and your everyday, uneventful, in-between.

Lord, help me to fix my thoughts on what is true, noble, right, pure, lovely, and admirable. Keep my heart guarded and secure in what is real and godly. Teach me to value what you are doing in the quiet moments of my journey. Thank You for walking with me, always.

In Jesus' Name, Amen.

When you think about who you are becoming, what qualities of Christ do you most want to reflect in your "everyday, uneventful, in-between"?

Lesson 33
WHEN WE ARE REAL, WE BEGIN TO HEAL

Not knocking the lashes, just needed to blink with nothing between me and God.

"Those who look to Him are radiant; their faces are never covered with shame."

Psalm 34:5

Please hear me, friend: I don't think there's anything wrong with wearing false eyelashes, hair extensions, or acrylic nails. If your heart and mind are in the right place, these things can simply be fun. They can serve as a creative expression and a compliment to who God made you to be.

I will always be a girly girl, but in my personal journey, there was a time when I needed to take a break from cosmetic extensions and all of the extras. During that time, the Lord was nudging me to let go of my "security blankets." I needed to learn that I would be just fine without a glamorous DCC look. You see, again and again I was fighting off the thought: "I'm just not good enough as I am."

It really wasn't about becoming more natural. It was about receiving healing. When I removed my hair extensions, eyelash extensions, and acrylic nails... what was left underneath needed a lot of healing. God used this example (in the physical) to show me (in the spiritual) what happens when we let Him remove our false security and let what is real... heal. Because sometimes our facades are admired by the world, but can end up being very costly and damaging to us.

Sometimes what looks great on the surface is actually hurting underneath. When you allow the real you to come into the light, you begin to heal. It takes time. And it's gonna feel naked, and "less than" for quite a while.

The Lord challenged me to let Him develop in me what He saw fit... not what the world said was successful. The scariest part for me was the misunderstanding and disapproval from others. But this scripture absolutely blew me away:

> "All those I dearly love I unmask and train. So repent and be eager to pursue what is right. Behold, I'm standing at the door, knocking. If your heart is open to hear my voice and you open the door within, I will come in to you and feast with you, and you will feast with me." - Revelation 3:19-20 (TPT)

Wow! For me, unmasking meant stripping away layers of protective walls, traditions, status symbols, false ideas, position, image, people pleasing.... and that was scary. But I came to realize that it wasn't my image, or anything of the sort, that made me valuable. I was still loved by God, *AND* as I unmasked, He worked through me to love and serve others more powerfully than ever before!

When God says to unmask, we will always experience beautiful freedom and a true closeness to Him that will far surpass the benefits of the mask we were hiding beneath.

So, I encourage you to search your heart and ask God: "Lord, in what ways do I need to unmask?" He can be trusted with your vulnerability. I promise that when you get real with Him and open the door to His presence, He will bring healing in every place you need it.

Lord, those who look to You are radiant; their faces are never covered with shame. Help me to come to You just as I am—honest, open, and real—knowing that Your love brings healing, not judgment. Shine Your light into every hidden place and make me whole again.

In Jesus' Name, Amen.

What "security blankets" or facades might God be inviting you to release so He can heal what's underneath?

Lesson 34
STORE UP TREASURES IN HEAVEN

An amazing sight, knowing that a steady flow of water over time, carved the mighty Grand Canyon.

"Do not store up for yourselves treasures on earth, where moths and vermin destroy, and where thieves break in and steal. But store up for yourselves treasures in heaven... For where your treasure is, there your heart will be also."

Matthew 6:19-21

As a DCC, I had the opportunity to take in a wide variety of experiences—about 90% of them, honestly, were incredible. But there's always that remaining 10% of stressful stuff that can chip away at you little by little. Sometimes it was the late-night rehearsals followed by early mornings at work. Other times it was last-minute changes right before stepping onto the field, navigating team dynamics, and handling public expectations with grace.

None of these things overshadowed the joy of the experience, but they were very real parts of it. They taught me something peculiar about myself: I handle big, dramatic circumstances better than the small, everyday stresses—the kind that don't seem like a big deal in the moment but add up over time, carving a canyon in my heart.

The big things push me straight into God's arms. There's no question that I need Him, and I cling to Him immediately. But with the little things, I tend to try and handle them myself. I let them linger in my thoughts, and I carry them way too long.

One day, I was feeling worn down by a series of those small things. So, I went for a bike ride by myself, trying to clear my head. I found myself replaying the stressful situations—over and over and over again. I finally cried out, "Dear Lord, why am I letting these things bother me so much?"

Straightaway, a picture of the Grand Canyon popped into my mind. I thought about how that massive canyon wasn't formed all at once—but by a steady stream of water over time. That's when it hit me: I was letting a flow of subtle worries and tension erode my heart.

I was amazed. I had gone through bigger things recently—and God had carried me through. But these little things? They stuck around and upset me even worse. Then the Holy Spirit gently pointed out: *"Where your treasure is, there your heart will be also."*

As I kept riding along on my bike, I felt a wave of encouragement rise in me. I realized something so freeing: I wanted to be in control... I actually treasured it. No wonder these uncontrollable circumstances carried so much weight. But God tenderly reminded me of His love and care for me, and that His ways are higher than my ways. Suddenly, my anxious thoughts lost their power.

I looked around at the vibrant green grass and brilliant blue sky—the vast beauty surrounding me—and I felt inspired. God is so big. These little worries? They're nothing in comparison.

I had a choice: I could let those small things keep carving away at my heart—or I could stop the erosion by refusing to give them any more power. I chose to place my treasure where it truly belongs: In heaven. With Him. In His greatness.

God knows the big picture. He's got you.

Don't let a need to "be in control" take away your peace... or His place in your heart.

I don't know what kind of discouragement you're facing today, but I know the enemy will use anything—small or large—to wear you down.

> **BUT GOD GENTLY REMINDED ME OF HIS LOVE AND CARE FOR ME, AND THAT HIS WAYS ARE HIGHER THAN MY WAYS. SUDDENLY, MY ANXIOUS THOUGHTS LOST THEIR POWER.**

So, I want to encourage you: Get alone with God. Let Him speak to your heart. Let Him give you a word that's just for you. Use His Word to fight back. *It is written.* That's how Jesus silenced the enemy. That's how we can too.

We don't have to let the slow trickle of worry wear us down anymore. We can dam it up with the truth of God's Word. Because our treasure is in heaven—and nothing on earth can touch it.

Lord, help me to release my desire for control. I recognize that I can trust You. Help me not to chase after treasures that fade, but to store up eternal riches with You. Turn my heart toward what truly matters—loving You, serving others, and living with eternity in mind. You are my treasure, and my heart is fully Yours.

In Jesus' Name, Amen.

What stressful, uncontrollable circumstances have you allowed to erode your heart over time—and what truth from God's Word can you speak over them today?

Lesson 35
MOVE BOLDLY TOWARD THE DREAMS GOD'S PLACED IN YOUR HEART

At the first DCC alumni reunion I attended, my precious boys were with me and so excited! I pray my boys will always move boldly toward the dreams God has placed in their hearts.

"For God has not given us a spirit of fear and timidity, but of power, love, and self-discipline."

2 Timothy 1:7

"I Hope You Dance" was a number-one song for Lee Ann Womack during my time with the Cowboys. It was more than just a beautiful melody—it was (and still is) a heartfelt invitation to say "yes" to life's opportunities, even when they feel uncertain or out of reach.

Becoming a Dallas Cowboys Cheerleader was stepping into a dream that once felt impossible—but God. If He calls you to it, He will also give you the courage and strength to walk it out. So today, I want to encourage you: Take the leap. Choose boldness over fear. Show up for your calling. And never stop dancing toward the dreams God has placed in your heart.

Let's reflect for a moment on the lyrics to that timeless song:

> "I hope you never lose your sense of wonder,
> You get your fill to eat but always keep that hunger,
> May you never take one single breath for granted,
> God forbid love ever leave you empty-handed.
> I hope you still feel small when you stand beside the ocean,
> Whenever one door closes, I hope one more opens.
> Promise me that you'll give faith a fighting chance,
> And when you get the choice to sit it out or dance—
> I hope you dance... I hope you dance.
> I hope you never fear those mountains in the distance,
> Never settle for the path of least resistance.
> Living might mean taking chances, but they're worth taking.
> Loving might be a mistake, but it's worth making.
> Don't let some hell-bent heart leave you bitter.
> When you come close to selling out—reconsider.
> Give the heavens above more than just a passing glance.
> And when you get the choice to sit it out or dance—
> I hope you dance... I hope you dance."
>
> *by Mark D. Sanders & Tia Sillers*

What a powerful and challenging message!

Before I sat down to write this lesson, I watched my sons head out the door and into the big ol' world. I thought about how many (hundreds) of times I've watched them venture into their day.

And how many times I've prayed this prayer over their hearts: "Lord, may their hearts bow to You. May their love for You increase their faith, strength, courage, integrity, and love for others."

I hope they "never settle for the path of least resistance." I hope no "hell-bent heart" ever leaves them bitter. I hope and pray they choose to dance.

And here's the truth: God gives all of us a chance to dance. But there will always be someone—or something—that tries to stop us. Why? Because the enemy of our souls wants to rob us—and the world—of what God created us to do. When we choose to dance—fully and freely—it glorifies God! So, of course, the enemy swoops in to oppose us. Sometimes people around us can unknowingly do his dirty work through bullying, discouragement, hatred, and mockery.

Everyone carries pain and insecurities. But we have a choice in how we handle ours: We can hurt others, or we can invite God to heal us.

When I look at my children and consider how God created them, I want them to dance with all their might! I pray they'll dance despite the enemy's discouragement. I believe God's purpose for their lives is so much greater than any opposition they'll face. So yes, I encourage them: "Promise me you'll give faith a fighting chance. And when you get the choice to sit it out or dance—I hope you dance."

If I *long* for this for my children, can you even imagine *how much God longs for us to dance*, His beloved children? Are you sitting it out right now? If so, I understand. I've been there. But consider these promises from Scripture:

> "Be strong and of good courage, do not fear nor be afraid of them; for the Lord your God, He is the One who goes with you. He will not leave you nor forsake you."
> - Deuteronomy 31:6

> "The Lord is my light and my salvation; whom shall I fear? The Lord is the strength of my life; of whom shall I be afraid?" - Psalm 27:1

> "You are the light of the world. A town built on a hill cannot be hidden. Neither do people light a lamp and put it under a bowl. Instead, they put it on its stand, and it gives light to everyone in the house. In the same way, let your light shine before others, that they may see your good deeds and glorify your Father in heaven."
> - Matthew 5:14–16

It's only by trusting Jesus that we ever gain the courage to truly let loose and dance. Just like David, who danced before the Lord with all his might, we can go all in—not holding back—and God will be glorified.

The ending lyrics of "I Hope You Dance" sum it all up so perfectly:

"Time is a wheel in constant motion always rolling us along/Tell me, who wants to look back on their years and wonder/Where those years have gone?"

I don't want to wonder.
I want to dance.
And I hope you dance, too.

Lord, thank You for giving me not a spirit of fear, but of power, love, and a sound mind. When life presents open doors and uncertain paths, help me step forward with courage and grace. Let me never sit out the dance of life, but trust You enough to move boldly toward the dreams You've placed in my heart.

In Jesus' Name, Amen.

Where in your life have you been "sitting out the dance" out of fear or uncertainty? What is one small, brave step you sense God nudging you to take this week?

Lesson 36
WITH GOD, WE OVERCOME THE WOUNDS OF WORDS

Just like a full cup overflows, what fills your heart will eventually pour out... choose carefully what you let in.

"He heals the brokenhearted and binds up their wounds."

Psalm 147:3

People sometimes say deeply cruel things, and for reasons we don't always understand, it can take a significant amount of time and effort to move beyond them.

During my DCC days, I learned what it was like to have a multitude of opinions coming my way. And that most people don't fully grasp the power of their words. Hurting people tend to hurt people. That's not an excuse—but it is an insight. Mean words are often the overflow of someone else's pain. They're not true. They come from a false, dark place.

We need to learn to delete those words from our "truth file." Send that junk straight to the trash! But let's be honest—just because we know hurtful words aren't true doesn't mean they don't hurt. That pain is real. And sometimes it's hard to shake. I understand.

From a young age, people repeatedly pointed out my physical imperfections:

"You're too short."
"Your body isn't proportioned right."
"Your hair is mousy and thin."
"You have 'problem skin.'"
"Buck teeth."
"A pug nose."
"You're too pale."
"You need to lose weight."

On and on it went. I felt... defective. So, I worked relentlessly to "fix" myself, trying desperately to measure up. I allowed my worth to be determined by others' opinions. And you know what? I believed them. I saw "truth" in every criticism. Then I'd compare myself to other girls—on TV, in magazines, on screen—and those same lies were echoed back to me by the world.

Living for the approval of others created a chain reaction of pain: insecurity, deep self-doubt, and eating disorders.

But here's the good news: Our God is a healer.

> *"He heals the brokenhearted and binds up their wounds." - Psalm 147:3*

If you've been hurt by words—more than you care to admit—I want to share three ways I've learned to overcome their impact:

1. Replace People's Words with God's Truth

Other people's opinions are no longer allowed to define you. God alone gets to give you your value.

This takes time—it's a renewal of the mind. Though I don't get it right every time, often when I'm tempted to believe the lie that my body type, etc., isn't good enough, I stop and replace it with truth:

> *I am fearfully and wonderfully made. - Psalm 139:14*

Satan would love for us to stay so wrapped up in insecurity that we never step into the bold life God created for us. That makes me mad just thinking about it!

Sometimes I literally say out loud: "Satan, you are a liar! You don't get to tell me who I am. God made me fearfully and wonderfully, and I will no longer believe your lies."

And a personal side note: I stopped reading fashion magazines and started reading God's Word instead. Best switch I ever made.

2. Forgive

This one's hard. But forgiveness is key to freedom. When we forgive, we release the hold those words—and those people—have had over us. We can't fully heal until we forgive completely.

Start by praying for the person who hurt you. It's nearly impossible to stay bitter toward someone you're sincerely praying for.

God's heart is for everyone to come to Him—even those who've been the cruelest. When we want healing and redemption for people who don't deserve it, our hearts begin to align with His.

3. Speak Life—to Others and to Yourself

God can heal any wound. But let's not be the reason someone else needs healing.

There is so much power in speaking words of encouragement and love—especially when you know what it feels like to receive the opposite. This is how we overcome evil with good.

It's a daily choice to break the cycle and defeat the enemy's plan. So talk kindly and respectfully to everyone AND to yourself. Speak life.

Now, here are three things NOT to do:

✗ 1. Agree with the Enemy

If you meditate long enough on everything negative others have said about you, you'll start to believe it. If you constantly tune in to the world's opinions and tune out God's Word, you will be deceived.

✗ 2. Suppress and Ignore Your Pain

Don't "stuff" your emotions or pretend they don't matter. Unforgiveness and bitterness can resurface later—through anxiety, depression, even physical sickness.

✗ 3. Return Fire with Fire

It might feel good for a moment to lash out, but in the end, it just causes more pain. Don't become what you hate.

Your Heavenly Father is crazy about you. He created you as His masterpiece—fearfully and wonderfully made. Seek the truth of who you are in Him, and watch the lies that were spoken over you fade into insignificance.

Lord, You heal the brokenhearted and bind up their wounds. I bring You the hurt caused by harsh words—whether they came from others or from my own mouth. Help me work with You to replace lies with truth, pain with peace, and bitterness with forgiveness. Teach me to speak words of life to others and to myself. Thank You for being the gentle healer of my soul.

In Jesus' Name, Amen.

What lie about yourself have you believed for too long? What truth from God's Word needs to take its place?

Lesson 37
FORGIVENESS IS GOD'S WAY

Speaking at Pure Joy Women's Conference on a subject very dear to my heart: Forgiveness.

"Do not repay evil for evil or reviling for reviling, but on the contrary, bless, for to this you were called, that you may obtain a blessing."

1 Peter 3:9

Being a Dallas Cowboys Cheerleader was a dream come true—but it came with intense pressure, constant scrutiny, and sometimes, real hurt. I learned how important it is to forgive quickly and fully. Holding onto offense just weighs you down. But forgiveness? It gives your spirit room to breathe again... to hope again... to live again.

And that lesson wasn't just for the cheerleading world. I've faced much deeper wounds—hurts that felt impossible to get over. But I've learned something powerful: The most influential person in your life is the one you refuse to forgive.

When we hold onto unforgiveness, we're the ones who become imprisoned. The enemy wants to keep us chained down in bitterness—but forgiveness breaks that chain. It's certainly not easy, but it's worth it. Forgiveness brings healing. It restores joy.

You might be thinking, "But you don't know what they did to me." You're right—I don't. But God does.

We've all been hurt in ways that are painfully unfair. But instead of holding onto the pain, God calls us to a better way. Scripture tells us to pray *against* evil—but to pray *for* the person who hurt us. Forgiveness may feel like letting the other person win. But it's actually how *you* win. It's an act of faith—believing that God sees it all and will handle the justice. He'll guide you in setting boundaries, and He'll give you the supernatural strength to forgive and move forward.

When we're the ones in need of forgiveness, God generously pours out His grace. And He calls us to extend that same grace to others. As we obey Him—by forgiving, praying for our enemies, and letting go of the hurt—our hearts begin to soften, and healing starts to take root.

Sometimes forgiveness leads to reconciliation. Other times, it means letting go and moving on. Either way, God is with you, and full freedom is possible!

Here are a few verses to help guide the journey:

"See that no one repays anyone evil for evil, but always seek to do good to one another and to everyone."
- 1 Thessalonians 5:15

"Bless those who persecute you... Do not be overcome by evil, but overcome evil with good."
- Romans 12:14 & 21

"Strive for peace with everyone... See to it that no root of bitterness springs up and causes trouble..."
- Hebrews 12:14–15

If there's any unforgiveness hiding in your heart today, bring it to God. Name the hurt. Acknowledge how it affected you. Then cancel the debt! Release it to God and let Him be your Defender. He will heal you—step by step, layer by layer. Don't miss the freedom waiting on the other side of forgiveness. Let Him make you stronger than ever before.

> **THE MOST INFLUENTIAL PERSON IN YOUR LIFE IS THE ONE YOU REFUSE TO FORGIVE.**

*Lord, Thank You for forgiving me with grace I don't deserve.
Help me extend that same grace to others, even when it's hard.
Free my heart from bitterness and fill it with Your love, so I can
live in the freedom You offer.*

In Jesus' Name, Amen.

*What offense or hurt have you been holding onto that still feels heavy?
What would it look like to place that weight into God's hands today?*

Lesson 38
ALWAYS SHOW GRATITUDE FOR YOUR FAMILY AND FRIENDS

This keepsake holds my dad, my mom, my sister, and me. It was a special gift from my friend Kaye Sharp, and a reminder to be grateful for family and friends who have shaped my life.

"Be devoted to one another in love. Honor one another above yourselves."

Romans 12:10

This wasn't just another performance. This was *the* performance—the one we looked forward to all year long. It wasn't about us in that moment. It was about them—the ones who cheered for the cheerleaders.

Our friends and family filled the room as we sang Broadway classics, belted out country hits, and performed the spectacular dances that had defined our season.

Every kick, every note, every smile was a giant "thank you" to the people who kept us grounded. The ones who prayed us through those exhausting rehearsals, lifted us up on hard days, and reminded us who we were underneath the glitz and glam.

We called it the "DCC Friends and Family Show," held at the beautiful Anatole Hotel in Dallas. Honestly? It felt like a giant group hug. No roaring stadium. No jumbotron. Just love and gratitude filling the air.

It reminded me of the old days, when I was a little girl putting on little shows for my family on the brick hearth in our living room—heart pounding, grinning from ear to ear, soaking in the joy of my people... the ones who mattered most.

Our DCC team had poured so much into this year, but none of us did it alone. God created us for community. And sometimes His greatest blessings come wrapped in the form of people—those quiet encouragers, ride-or-die friends, parents who show up (again and again), or someone who believes in you even when you're not so sure yourself.

As I looked out into the audience that day, I saw my parents, my sister and her family, my soon-to-be husband and his family, and my sweet, loyal friends. My heart could've burst. They had walked with me every step of the way—and I knew I couldn't have made it without them.

And in that moment, I was reminded of our ultimate encourager—Jesus. Even when the "boots" we've stepped into feel a few sizes too big, or the "dance" we're trying to learn feels way too complicated,

He's right there... cheering us on. Through Him, we learn how to love big, give generously, and keep going even when it's tough.

So, here's your friendly reminder: Take a moment today to thank the people who've stood by you, rooted for you, and helped you become who you are. And most of all, thank The Lord—the One who never leaves your side, your greatest encourager, and the source of all strength and grace.

Lord, thank You for the people You've placed in my life to lift me up, cheer me on, and remind me of my purpose. Help me to honor them well and to be that same support for others. Thank You for being my constant source of strength and encouragement.

In Jesus' Name, Amen.

Where do you sense Jesus cheering you on in this current season? How is He inviting you to rely on His strength?

Lesson 39
GIVE YOUR BEST YES

At every fork in the road, ask God for your "best yes."

"If any of you lacks wisdom, you should ask God, Who gives generously to all without finding fault, and it will be given to you."

James 1:5

Do you ever feel like you're standing at a fork in the road… and it's time to choose… not between good and bad, but between good and best? Yeah? Me too.

When Jerod and I started planning our wedding and dreaming about our future together, I realized that trying out for another season as a Dallas Cowboys Cheerleader would stretch us past our limits. I wanted to say "yes" to everything—but I had to learn how to give my "best yes" (a wise truth and catchy phrase my dear friend Haley taught me).

Becoming a DCC wasn't just something I did; it was something I loved. It was an experience chock-full of life-changing lessons that affected every part of my existence. I had battled for so many years to become a DCC, and I understood *to my core* that it was a once-in-a-lifetime opportunity. Choosing not to audition again was painful. But after much prayer, I knew God was inviting me to turn the page.

I was walking away from something good… but I was stepping toward what was best: the life God was building with Jerod and the new purposes He had prepared for us.

Sometimes giving your "best yes" means releasing something precious so you can fully embrace what's next. It takes trust. It takes faith. And it definitely takes surrender. But every time we say "yes" to God's way, He leads us into deeper joy, fuller peace, and a purpose that's more fulfilling than anything we could've dreamed up ourselves.

And that lesson isn't just for the big, life-changing moments. I'm learning it in the everyday ones too. Take laundry, for example. (Yes—laundry. Stay with me.)

I have this tendency to cram three loads' worth of clothes into one. Efficiency, right? Except, instead of that fresh "ocean breeze" or "lavender serenity" scent, I end up with something like… "damp gym socks and disappointment." So, what do I do? I either hit "re-wash" or just wear the clothes, anyway, grinning and bearing with the lingering aroma. Not exactly a success story!

Well, one day I reached for a towel, and it smelled amazing. Like—I think I heard angels singing. Turns out, Jerod had done that load.

He didn't rush. He didn't overload the machine. He just did one load, the right way. Imagine that! As silly as it sounds, God used it to remind me: When life feels overloaded, even with good things, it's time to ask, "What can I let go of so I can give my best to what God has really called me to do?"

Whether it's laundry or life choices, the principle is the same: You can't do everything. But with God's wisdom, you can do the right things. The best things. And it's more than OK to politely say to people, "No, thank you." Or, "Not at this time."

So today, I encourage you—ask the Lord for wisdom. He promises to give it generously. Whether you're standing at a major life crossroads or just staring at an overloaded to-do list, He'll show you how to give your "best yes."

Lord, help me to trust You in every decision—big or small. Teach me how to let go of what's just "good," so I can say "yes" to what's best. Thank You that Your plans are always beneficial, and that when I follow You, You'll lead me to peace, purpose... and maybe even a perfectly fresh towel.

In Jesus' Name, Amen.

What "three-loads-in-one" area of your life feels crammed, rushed, or overloaded right now? What's one thing you could let go of this week to create room for peace?

Lesson 40

YOU ARE ENOUGH IN CHRIST JESUS

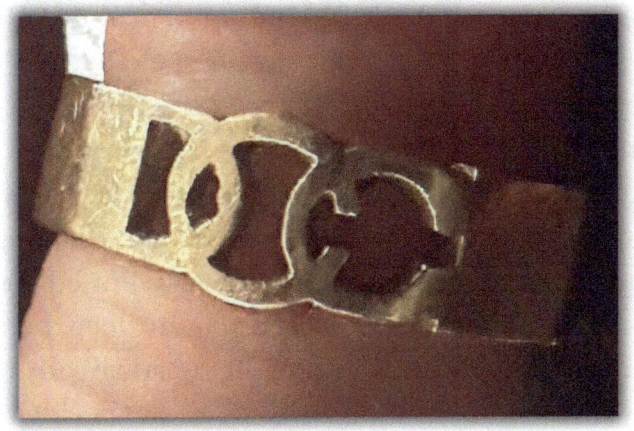

A small ring, a big reminder: I can do all things through Christ who strengthens me.

"The Lord your God wins victory after victory, and is always with you. He celebrates and sings because of you, and He will refresh your life with His love."

Zephaniah 3:17 (CEV)

I looked down and saw the gold pinky ring on my hand—the one I had been given at our "DCC End of Year Banquet." That tiny circle meant I had *made it*. I would always be a part of the sisterhood, but it represented so much more than that. The fact that I actually received it pointed to how God had carried me, strengthened me, refined me, and blessed me in my lengthy pursuit of becoming a Dallas Cowboys Cheerleader. There's no doubt, if I had been the one orchestrating my journey, it would have looked very different—without the struggles, detours, and defeats. But I can sincerely say, I am grateful for the way God wove together every moment—the victories and the setbacks—into life-changing lessons. He used it all for the good... like only He can. Even if I had never made the team, I still would have gained the greatest gift: knowing Jesus' love and grace on a much deeper level. Today, I stand in awe of His faithfulness and all He has done in my life since.

Just recently, my husband and I took a walk through the neighborhood in Branson, Missouri where I'd lived as a young twenty-something. I hadn't set foot in those old stomping grounds for years, but I felt compelled to return. As we huffed and puffed up the hills, memory after memory rose from the deep, breaking the surface of my mind. In that season of life, I had already heard "no" twice to my dream of becoming a DCC. I hadn't decided if I could muster up the courage to try again. My heart was heavy with rejection, yet I was right in the middle of learning what it meant to receive God's unconditional love.

With vivid clarity, I remembered how I used to feel back then—so unsure of myself and weighed down by the thought: "I am not enough." I hadn't quite grasped the truth yet: In myself, I am not enough, but in Christ Jesus, I am more than enough.

As I waked and reflected on those days, I realized I was on a slow, back-and-forth exploration of learning to trust God's Word—not just by reading it, but by committing to *believe it* and *live it*. Along the way, I discovered that Scripture holds the answers to the very questions our souls ache to understand:

Am I loved? Am I worth knowing? Do I matter? Is there really a good purpose for my life?

Before I knew how to bring those questions to God, I kept handing them to people—hoping someone could fulfill me: You're enough. You're valuable. You're seen. But when I began to learn who I was in Christ—and to actually believe His Word in my heart—those longings were answered, little by little, in the power of His love.

If I could sit down with that younger version of myself—and if I could sit with you today, face to face—I would look you in the eyes and say this:

God chose you before the foundations of the world. He knit you together in your mother's womb. Before you ever took your first breath, He already loved you. He created your innermost being and cherishes you beyond measure. He knows every thought you think. He's counted every hair on your head. He's caught every tear you've cried.

You are not an accident. You are not a burden. You are His—handcrafted with love, made in the image of the Creator Himself. That means you're not only special to Him… you're sacred. You are His masterpiece.

And here's what's even more incredible: There is nothing—absolutely nothing—you could ever do to lose His love. And there's nothing you have to do in order to keep it.

God's love for you is so immense that He gave His only Son, Jesus, to redeem you. By believing in Him, you receive eternal life and will *never perish*. Then as His beloved child, your inheritance is every spiritual blessing in Christ. His Spirit will live inside of you, empowering you to walk in your God-given purpose. And His thoughts toward you? They are endless, deeper than you could ever imagine.

He is the lover of your soul. The One who rejoices over you with singing. The One who will quiet your anxious heart with His love.

The One who will never leave, never grow tired of you, and never stop pursuing your heart.

You don't have to chase love anymore—it's already chasing you.

You don't have to prove your worth—it was already proven at the cross.

You don't have to be enough for everyone—you're already enough in Christ Jesus.

How do I know? Because these truths are written in His Word. And once I began to believe what He says, everything changed. I don't have to earn love anymore. I can freely give it—even if it isn't returned—because I'm no longer pouring from emptiness but from overflow. Jesus is my source, and He is always more than enough. In my weakness, His strength shines through, and with Him I can truly do all things I'm called to do.

So, as I stood at the top of the hill in my old neighborhood, looking back at where I used to be, I simply praised God. He never left me. He never gave up on me. He healed me, restored me, and renewed my mind. Tears filled my eyes as I worshipped Him. Jesus is the way, the truth, and the life! To know Him as Lord and Savior and to receive His Word as the bread of life is a priceless gift—ours to embrace, treasure, and live by, today and always. Praise His Holy Name!

In Him we are enough.

Prayer

Lord, You are amazing! Thank You for covering me in your righteousness and for quieting my heart with Your unconditional love. I don't just want to seek Your hand—I want to seek Your heart. You are my treasure, and I love You with all of my heart, soul, mind and strength!

In Jesus' Name, Amen.

Reflection

How might Jesus be inviting you to see yourself through His eyes instead of your own? From this day forward, will you commit to seek Jesus with all your heart… and believe that in Him, you are more than enough?

FIRST STEPS IN WALKING WITH JESUS

Dear cherished reader,

Thank you for allowing me to share my stories, my struggles, and the lessons I've learned along the way with you. Maybe something in these pages stirred something deeper in you. Maybe you're wondering what it would look like to really know Jesus—not just know about Him, but to walk with Him.

You were made for a relationship with Him—not religion, not performance, not pressure. A real relationship, rooted in love and anchored in truth.

The Bible says that God demonstrates His love for us in this: While we were still sinners, Christ died for us—to save us (Romans 5:8). Salvation is a gift from God—completely undeserved, unearned, and given freely by His grace. We receive it by placing our faith in Jesus Christ alone—not by our own efforts or good works (Ephesians 2:8–9).

Jesus gave His life to redeem us. When we believe in Him, His work on the cross gives us eternal life with Him in heaven, along with true peace, lasting hope, and a fresh start—not someday, but today.

If you're ready to take that step and place your trust in Jesus, you can begin with a simple, heartfelt prayer like this:

Jesus, I believe You are the Son of God. I believe You died for my sins and rose again to give me life. I know I cannot save myself, and I place my trust in You alone for my salvation. Please forgive me, change me, and lead me. From this day forward, I want to follow You with all my heart. I give You my life.

In Your powerful Name, Jesus, Amen!

If you have placed your trust in Jesus and turned to Him in faith, all of heaven is rejoicing—and so am I! (Luke 15:7).

You are now a new creation in Christ (2 Corinthians 5:17), saved by grace through faith, and nothing will ever separate you from His love (Romans 8:38–39).

This is just the beginning.

When we seek the Lord with all our heart, He promises we will find Him (Jeremiah 29:13). He is the treasure your heart has longed for. So, I encourage you to keep seeking Him. Stay grounded in His Word. Find a Bible-believing church. Surround yourself with believers who will walk this faith journey with you.

And always remember:
You are deeply loved, fully known, and forever His.

I have prayed for you as I've written these pages, and I will always be praying Ephesians 3:16-20 for you:

"I pray that out of His glorious riches He may strengthen you with power through His Spirit in your inner being, so that Christ may dwell in your hearts through faith. And I pray that you, being rooted and established in love, may have power, together with all the Lord's holy people, to grasp how wide and long and high and deep is the love of Christ, and to know this love that surpasses knowledge—that you may be filled to the measure of all the fullness of God. Now to Him who is able to do immeasurably more than all we ask or imagine, according to His power that is at work within us, to Him be the glory in the church and in Christ Jesus throughout all generations, for ever and ever! Amen."

Welcome to the family!

With love and celebration,

Carolyn Clifton Hill

About the Author

Carolyn Clifton Hill is a former Dallas Cowboys Cheerleader who lived out her dream during the unforgettable era of Troy Aikman, Emmitt Smith, and Deion Sanders. She spent several years, both before and after her time on the squad, performing in multiple music shows in Branson, Missouri, and Pigeon Forge, Tennessee.

Today, Carolyn's greatest passion is sharing Jesus. She loves leading worship, encouraging ladies through Pure Joy women's conferences, and serving in women's ministry at her church. Whether on a stage or in a small group, she loves helping others find joy, hope, and identity in Christ.

Carolyn lives in Branson, MO and is married to her favorite travel partner, Dr. Jerod Hill. They are blessed with two amazing sons, Connor and Dylan. She considers faith and family her greatest treasures and is grateful for every opportunity to share God's goodness with others.

You can learn more about Carolyn at carolyncliftonhill.com.

Made in the USA
Coppell, TX
07 January 2026